Loyal Opposition

A Christian Response to the Clinton Agenda

by John Eidsmoe

HUNTINGTON HOUSE PUBLISHERS

Huntington House Publishers
P.O. Box 53788
Lafayette, LA 70505

Library of Congress Card Catalog Number
93-78388
ISBN 1-56384-044-8

Dedication

This book is somewhat roguishly dedicated to those Christians who, either by voting for Bill Clinton or by failing to vote for George Bush, made the Clinton Agenda possible and this book necessary.

"Righteousness exalteth a nation: but sin is a reproach to any people."

Proverbs 14:34

"If the foundations be destroyed, what can the righteous do?"

Psalm 11:3

"When the righteous are in authority, the people rejoice: but when the wicked beareth rule, the people mourn."

Proverbs 29:2

"If my people, which are called by my name, shall humble themselves, and pray, and seek my face, and turn from their wicked ways; then will I hear from heaven, and will forgive their sin, and will heal their land."

2 Chronicles 7:14

Acknowledgments

I gratefully acknowledge the assistance of Mark Anthony, Reneé Cazayoux, Renatti Dupont, Laura England, and all of the staff at Huntington House for their inspiration, diligence, cooperation and patience in the production of this book.

Contents

Chapter 1   Loyal Opposition: Is It a Matter of   7
             Right or Wrong?

Chapter 2   Bill and Hillary Clinton: Politically   25
             Correct or Biblically Correct?

Chapter 3   Did God Vote for Bill Clinton?   57

Chapter 4   *Loyal* Opposition: The Role   65
             of Loyalty

Chapter 5   Loyal *Opposition*: The Role of   77
             Opposition

Chapter 6   A Victory Plan for Conservative   90
             Christians during the Clinton Era

Appendix   126

Notes   158

chapter 1

Loyal Opposition: Is It a Matter of Right or Wrong?

If God told you to vote for Bill Clinton, would you do it?

I suppose I would, but first I'd insist upon some identification (to be assured that the Person speaking is truly God).

When God speaks, He is a difficult person to argue with—because He is always right.

With others we use reason, emotion, and evidence, disputing and evaluating each other's points. But once God speaks, the argument is over. He is right, because He is the final authority, the author of right.

God has been known to speak through a burning bush, through angels, or through the clouds in communicating His will to men. But most often He has chosen to communicate to people through people.

The person who speaks for God, therefore, carries great authority, his words carrying divine authority and being indisputable.

But the person who claims to speak for God also carries great responsibility. What if he doesn't really speak for God? What if he is engaged in planned deception, or is deceived himself? God doesn't take such matters lightly. As He said through Moses over three thousand years ago

> . . . but the prophet, which shall presume to speak a word in my name, which I have not commanded him to speak or that shall speak in the name of other gods, even that prophet shall die. (Deut. 18:20)

Nor do God's people take such matters lightly. Moses posed the question, "How may we know the word which the Lord has not spoken?" (Deut. 18:21). He then gave the answer:

> When a prophet speaketh in the name of the Lord, if the thing follow not, nor come to pass, that is the thing which the Lord hath not spoken, but the prophet hath spoken it presumptuously: thou shalt not be afraid of him. (Deut. 18:22)

The fact that the prophet was deceived and sincerely believed God had spoken to him was no defense. He had the duty to be sure he was right before claiming to speak for the Lord. In those days people took very seriously the danger of error in matters concerning the Word of God.

Christians and Jews have traditionally believed that God can and does speak to man. He spoke through His revealed Word, the Bible, and before Scripture was complete He spoke through other men by means of dreams, visions, direct words, angels, theophanic appearances like the pillar of fire or the burning bush. Some Christians believe God still speaks new revelation to people today.

But Christians and Jews are not the only people who believe in divine revelation. In the ancient world the Canaanites and other pagan people believed Baal, Moloch, and other pagan divinities spoke to them during wild sex orgies and other rituals. More recently Joseph Smith (founder of Mormonism), Mary Baker Eddy (Christian Science), C. T. Russell (Jehovah's Witnesses), and Sun Myung Moon (Unification Church) have all claimed that God spoke through them and therefore they speak for God.

With this in mind, we must therefore evaluate prophets and prophecies carefully. If genuinely from God, they must be accepted as true. But if false, they can lead many into serious error—and a sincere but misguided prophet can be just as dangerous as an intentional deceiver.

It would be helpful if every false prophet wore a sign saying, "Beware of Me! I Am a False Prophet!" But that isn't likely to happen. Many false prophets are sincerely deceived, and intentional deceivers certainly aren't going to give away their game.

So when someone claims to speak for God, how do we evaluate his claim? "Beloved, believe not every spirit, but try the spirits whether they are of God: because many false prophets are gone out into the world" (1 John 4:1). But how do we "try" spirits?

The Bible gives us several tests, the first of which is in the next verse of the passage:

> Hereby know ye the Spirit of God: Every spirit that confesseth that Jesus Christ is come in the flesh is of God: And every spirit that confesseth not that Jesus

Christ is come in the flesh is not of God: and this is
that spirit of antichrist, whereof ye have heard that it
should come; and even now already is it in the world.
(1 John 4:2-3)

The first test, then, is: Does the alleged prophet
believe in the incarnation of Jesus Christ?

Second, we compare his message with that which we
know to be the Word of God, the Bible. If the alleged
prophet's message is contrary to the Bible correctly
interpreted and applied, the prophet's message must be
rejected as false.

Third, we compare the alleged prophet's message to
that which we see around us—reality as we know it. As
we have seen, the Israelites put their prophets to a very
strict test. If the prophecy came to pass in every respect,
the prophet probably spoke for God. But if he was
wrong in *any* detail, his message must be rejected as
false; for God never errs, even though Satan sometimes
speaks a partial truth.

Fourth, we evaluate the alleged prophet's message
in the light of common sense and ordinary reason. True,
revelation can sometimes supersede reason. But God
gave us the power of reason as a means of apprehending truth, and while revelation may sometimes supersede reason, it does not contradict reason.

Fifth, we look at the alleged prophet himself. Certainly God uses imperfect human instruments to communicate His will; otherwise He wouldn't use any of us.
But when a person claims to speak for God, it is appropriate to ask, *Has this person given reliable information in
the past? And are there reasons to believe he may be biased
or deceived today, or that he may have a motive for deceiving
others?*

Enter Paul Cain.

On 2 November 1992, Paul Cain claims to have had
a dream. In this dream God told Cain that Bill Clinton
would be elected president the following day.

As confirmation, Cain says, God showed him the headlines that would appear in five major newspapers Wednesday morning announcing Clinton's election.

At 10:30 A.M., Tuesday 3 November, Cain says he wrote a letter to Rick Joyner telling him about the dream and the headlines. Joyner claims to have the envelope postmarked 3 November and the letter from Cain.

For several days thereafter, Cain says, the Lord continued to give him revelations about the upcoming Clinton administration. Cain and Joyner discuss these revelations in an article which appeared in the *Morning Star Prophetic Bulletin*, January 1993.

The basic thrust of these revelations is that "the Lord loves and intends to use Bill Clinton. The Lord does not see him as he is, but as the man he will become. This is why the church must respond to Mr. Clinton's election by obeying the Biblical command to pray for him" (p. 2).

Many evangelical Christians were skeptical of Clinton's candidacy, questioning his character and believing his positions on key issues like abortion and homosexuality to be contrary to the principles found in the Bible. Cain and Joyner acknowledge these problems, but they insist, "In many ways it is better to have wrong doctrine with humility than to have right doctrine with pride. If a man with wrong doctrine has humility the Lord can change him. Bill Clinton has a humility that the Lord can reach and use" (pp. 2-3).

Cain and Joyner say of this revelation,

The most amazing and wonderful aspect of this dream was that Paul Cain saw the Lord putting His Spirit upon Bill Clinton and changing him into another man, just as He did King Saul in I Samuel!

Why did the Lord choose Bill Clinton? Because He intends to put His Spirit upon him and make him into a new man. He is going to give him the power of the Holy Spirit to lead this country. What some people in the church regarded as a defeat is actually a blessing from the Lord. If the church will pray for this it will come to pass. (p. 2)

Cain and Joyner are highly critical of conservative evangelical leaders, whom they say have a "spirit of intolerance that is potentially more dangerous than the moral issues they so vehemently oppose" (p. 3). Applying Proverbs 6:16-19 ("These six things doth the Lord hate: yea, seven are an abomination unto him . . .") to conservative evangelicals, Cain and Joyner say church leaders are guilty of pride and resentment, lying, hatred, poisoning people against their leaders, seeing only the evil and not the good in the Clinton administration, and spreading strife among Christians. Such charges deserve comment, though not a detailed refutation. Certainly evangelical Christians have the same sinful nature as everyone else, and certainly they can and should profit from constructive criticism. But the charges of pride and resentment are not supported or detailed in any way; a belief in absolute values does not necessarily constitute pride, nor is abhorrence of evil necessarily resentment or hatred. Cain and Joyner give no evidence of evangelical Christian leaders lying. The charge of poisoning people against their leaders could be applied to the Old Testament prophets who criticized Israel's apostate kings, or to Jesus for His scathing criticisms of the scribes and pharisees, or to Cain and Joyner for their criticism of evangelical leaders. Many of us would like to find something good about the Clinton administration (Cain and Joyner have shown us nothing except Bill Clinton's supposed "humility"); and the accusation of spreading strife among Christians could just as easily be applied to Cain and Joyner as to the Christian leaders they criticize.

Cain and Joyner also question whether the church should be involved in fighting moral evil by means of civil legislation, arguing that "morality instituted by compulsion can only be maintained by increasing control and fear" (p. 3). Technically this is true; we enforce murder statutes by threatening and imposing severe penalties for murder. This is the biblical role of civil government, to be God's "revenger to execute wrath upon him that doeth evil" (Rom. 13:4). Cain and Joyner seem to feel the church has gone too far in seeking legislation against moral evil, and argue that we should work for national repentance and revival instead.

Cain and Joyner believe God will use President Clinton to unify America regionally, racially, and economically (p. 7), but whether God succeeds in His plan for President Clinton depends upon the church: "The Lord stated to Paul Cain in his dream that it was His intention to use Clinton for good and not for evil, but it will depend on how the church responds to him" (p. 2).

In other words, if Cain's prophecy does not come to pass, it will be the church's fault for not rallying behind the Clinton administration.

How do we then evaluate Paul Cain's "vision"? Is it truly of God?

Anyone can claim to have received a revelation. I could claim (though I hasten to add, I do not) that God revealed to me in a vision that Paul Cain's vision is false, or that his interpretation of the vision is mistaken. On what basis would one claim that my "vision" is false and Cain's is true, or that Cain's "vision" is false and mine is true?

It might be possible that God plans to change and use Bill Clinton as Cain describes, though this would not necessarily mean that God has communicated this knowledge to Paul Cain in a vision. But we must consider the matter of human volition as well. Does God change leaders as though they were robots? Would He change Bill Clinton if Clinton is unwilling to change?

And we must consider another possibility—that dark spiritual powers plan to use the Clinton administration to implement their agenda of abortion, gay rights, etc. They may perceive the church as a major obstacle standing in their path. If so, they may try to neutralize the church's opposition to the Clinton agenda. Would not a "vision" like this, advising Christians that they should support the Clinton administration because God says so, be an ideal way to divide the church and neutralize its opposition?

So once again, how do we evaluate Paul Cain's vision? Logically there are several possibilities:

(1) Cain received a vision from the Lord and has interpreted it correctly.

(2) Cain received a vision from the Lord, but his interpretation of the vision is incorrect, in whole or in part.

(3) Cain has received a supernatural vision, but it was not from God. If the vision was not from God or elect angels acting at God's direction, it must have been from Satan or his demons. If so, Cain may or may not be aware of the true source of his vision. He may know it is demonic, or he may be deceived into believing the vision is of God. After all, Satan is capable of transforming himself into an "angel of light" (2 Cor. 11:14-15).

(4) Cain did not receive a vision from the Lord, but sincerely believes he did and is deceived by his own imagination.

(5) Cain did not receive a vision from the Lord, knows he did not receive any such vision, and is engaged in a planned deception to which Joyner may or may not be a party.

(6) Cain ate too much spicy food that Monday night.

Which of these possibilities is most likely? (I'll lump number six in with number four.) This book will not provide a definitive answer to this question. Nor will I attack the characters or motives of Paul Cain and Rick Joyner, though of course, anyone who claims to speak for the Lord through direct revelation must of necessity open his character and motives for examination.

Suffice it to say that I do not believe Paul Cain has correctly interpreted the will of God on this matter.

Cain and Joyner apparently believe the fulfillment of Cain's prediction of the Wednesday morning headlines demonstrates that the vision is truly of God. This is not necessarily true, although it might eliminate possibility four—that the vision was a delusion of Cain's imagination.

The fulfilled headlines do not eliminate the possibility of planned deception. There are at least two ways such a fraud could have been perpetrated.

First, how do we know Paul Cain sent the letter to Rick Joyner on 3 November? Is the word of Cain and Joyner sufficient? It is difficult and unpleasant to question the word of a man who claims to speak for God, but in dealing with matters of spiritual truth one cannot be too careful.

In addition to the word of Cain and Joyner, we also have the letter, and the envelope with the 3 November postmark. But how do we know the letter was sent in the 3 November envelope? How do we know it wasn't supplied later? Here we have only the word of Cain and Joyner.

But if Cain sent the envelope 3 November, and then supplied the letter later, Joyner would know that. If a fraud was perpetrated in this manner, Joyner would have to be a party to it. Is there any way Cain could have pulled off such a hoax by himself?

It might be possible. When was the letter sent? Cain says he wrote down the headlines about 10:30 A.M. Tuesday, 3 November, but all we know for certain is that envelope was postmarked sometime before midnight Tuesday night. By midnight Tuesday the results of the election had been known for several hours, and with a few well-placed phone calls or connections the Wednesday morning headlines might easily have been determined. It might even be possible that tentative headlines had been determined earlier than that, assuming a Clinton win.

Even if we concede that the headlines could not have been predicted by human intelligence alone, that doesn't prove the vision was of God. Satan and his demons sometimes give prophetic visions to deceive people and lead them to rely upon the occult.

As a created being, Satan is not all-knowing like God, and he does not see the future as the "eternal now" the way God does. But he is very intelligent, and he has had thousands of years of experience in observing human nature and watching human events. With the aid of his demons he also has great access to current information. He is therefore able to predict future events with considerable accuracy, though not with the unfailing accuracy of God.

That is one reason God directed His people to evaluate their prophets with a strict test that would distinguish the considerable accuracy of Satan's prophets from the 100 percent accuracy of a true prophet of God.

So whence came Paul Cain's vision—from God, from Satan, or from his own imagination? Let us consider the dream and subsequent revelations in light of the criteria mentioned at the beginning of this chapter.

First, when we compare the vision to the infallible standard, the Bible, the vision falls short. It is true that God's Word commands us to pray for our leaders (1 Tim. 2:1-2) and to obey civil authority (Rom. 13:1-7; 1 Pet. 2:13-17), except where civil authority contradicts the clear commands of God (Acts 5:29). But we are also told to resist evil (1 Pet. 5:9) and to earnestly contend for the faith (Jude 3). The Old Testament prophets did not hesitate to criticize the kings, judges, and other civil authorities when they engaged in wickedness or acted contrary to the Word of God.

Second, we look to reality as we see it around us and determine whether the prophet's vision corresponds to reality by coming to pass in every respect (Deut. 18:20). As noted earlier, Cain and Joyner claim the vision is authenticated by the five Wednesday morning newspaper headlines which were revealed in a dream Monday night. But the only proof of this is a Tuesday postmark, and the headlines could have been known by midnight Tuesday. Furthermore, while four of the headlines were apparently predicted accurately, the *Atlanta Constitution* actually headlined its story "Clinton Seeks Reunited States," while Cain predicted it would read simply "Reunited States." Under the strict standard of accuracy employed by the Hebrews, this discrepancy alone might be sufficient to discredit the prophecy, for the Hebrews were very careful to ensure that their prophets did in fact speak for God.

And while the Clinton administration is still in its beginning stages, early events do not confirm Cain's vision. Cain and Joyner declare that God "intends to put His Spirit upon him [Clinton] and make him into a new man. He is going to give him the power of the Holy Spirit to lead this country. What some people in the church regard as a defeat is actually a blessing from the Lord" (p. 2).

But far from being a "blessing from the Lord," the early days of the Clinton administration have been a far greater disaster than most Christians ever imagined. As chapter 3 will demonstrate, the Clinton administration opened its agenda with sweeping new policies allowing federally funded programs to advocate abortion, permitting abortions at military hospitals, seeking to allow homosexuals in the armed forces, appointing many far Left figures to cabinet and subcabinet positions, and promising to nominate a pro-abortion candidate to fill the new vacancy on the Supreme Court. It is of course possible that God might change Clinton in the future, but I see no sign of that happening thus far.

Remember, too, that President Clinton and his aides are not robots. While God can and does influence and change public officials, they are responsible moral agents. God will not bend their volition beyond certain limits. In other words, God is not likely to change Clinton unless Clinton is willing to be changed.

Note, however, that Cain and Joyner have left themselves an easy "out": "If the church will pray for this it will come to pass" (p. 2). If the prophecy doesn't come to pass, Cain and Joyner can always say the fault lies with the conservative church for failing to heed Cain's vision and pray sufficiently for the Clinton administration.

Third, is Paul Cain's vision credible in the light of common sense and ordinary reason? Cain and Joyner say, "The Lord showed Paul Cain that some of the characteristics in Bill Clinton that were interpreted as 'waffling on the issues' were really a genuine openness and desire to do what is right and fair" (p. 2).

Does humility seem to be the underlying motive behind those who waffle on issues—particularly when the waffling seems prompted by a desire to please a particular crowd or constituency, or to dodge embarrassing pointed questions from the media?

What signs of humility do President and Hillary Clinton display? Does the Clinton administration show signs of seeking the will of God in political matters? Does past experience indicate that a candidate for public office who takes the liberal position on virtually every issue is likely to do an about-face and espouse biblical values once he is elected?

And by contrast, does belief in moral values, which transcend man himself, constitute evidence of pride? A sense of conviction about the truth of God's Word is not necessarily arrogance.

Certainly there may be depths of humility in President Clinton's character that we have not seen to date. But thus far, common sense does not indicate that Paul Cain's prophecy will prove to be valid.

Finally, what about Paul Cain himself? Have his other prophecies proven reliable? Is he likely to be deceived, or does he have a motive for deceiving others?

Paul Cain is a charismatic evangelical who has in the past been associated with Kansas City Fellowship (KCF), a group known for its energetic charismatic emphasis. For some time, Cain and KCF had the endorsement of John Wimber of the Vineyard church network. But according to Lee Grady in *Charisma*, February 1993,

> Wimber now says he has decided to end any official relationship with Paul Cain. According to Wimber, "[Cain] has no role in the Vineyard other than being my friend. We have a wonderful relationship. I just do not feel called to promote his eschatological focus." (*Charisma*, p. 64)

Why did Wimber and Vineyard choose to end their relationship with Paul Cain? Apparently Cain's teachings and prophecies have created controversy in the past. As Grady says in *Charisma*, "The controversy became more heated three years ago when Ernest Gruen, a charismatic pastor in Shawnee, Kan., aired public accusations that Cain [and others] were spreading heresy" (*Charisma*, p. 64).

John Armstrong writes in *Power Religion* (Michael Scott Horton, ed. Chicago: Moody Press, 1992, p. 66) that Paul Cain "began receiving angelic visits at age eight. A high point of Cain's testimony is his claim that Jesus materialized in his (that is Cain's) Lincoln automobile during the 1950s to inform him that He was jealous of the prophet's fiancée and to command him to remain single and celibate for the rest of his life."

Armstrong writes further,

> Cain was also an associate of the healer-evangelist William Branham, who received revelations from an angel, too. Among those revelations were the following: the doctrine of the Trinity is "a doctrine of demons"; Eve's sin involved sexual relations with the serpent, but the "seed of God" were Branham's followers, otherwise known as "the Bride" or "the New Breed" (popular designations in the "Latter Rain" version of Pentecostalism). Furthermore, Branham

claimed himself the angel of Revelation 3:14 and
10:7, eventually baptizing people into his own name
and leading others to do the same. Branham proph-
esied that by 1977 all denominations would be sub-
sumed under the World Council of Churches, which
would be under the control of the Roman Catholic
Church. (p. 66)

And yet, Paul Cain declared that "William Branham
was the greatest prophet in the 20th century." Asked
how he could make such a statement despite Branham's
blatant heresies, Cain answered that such errors were
"such a small part of his presentation that it just swept
by everyone, until it became his pet theology," and that
his assessment of Branham's greatness was not due to
Branham's doctrines but to "his gifting in the word of
knowledge" (pp. 66-67). Such a lack of discernment in
Cain's assessment of Branham certainly casts doubt upon
Cain's credibility as a prophet.

In December 1992 Paul Cain met personally with
President-elect Clinton. Speaking at Abundant Life Fellowship in Mt. Gilead, Ohio, in March 1993, Cain said
his meeting with Clinton

went extremely well. And the Lord has called me to
be President Clinton's friend, and as a friend I can't
discuss what took place that evening between us, but
I can say this much. I said to the President, "I'm glad
that the Lord called me to love you and to stand by
you before I knew what your policies were, because
when I found out what your policies were, I was
stunned."

Cain then emphasized his opposition to abortion
and homosexuality, but one wonders why he was unaware of Clinton's well-publicized views on these subjects before. One suspicion is that Cain may be a well-

meaning but politically naive person who is being ma-nipulated by forces he doesn't really understand.

More recently, Cain's ministry seems to have as-sumed an international character. In his Abundant Life speech, Cain said that "towards the end of the last year [1992] the Lord spoke to me clearly as I was hanging out my ordination plaque or ordination certificate and my doctor of divinity degree. . . . The Lord says 'You won't need that, because I'm going to make you a D.D.—Divine Diplomat.'" This means, Cain said, that "the Lord has called me to represent the purposes of the Kingdom of God before international leaders."

Early in February 1993, Cain said, he went to Iraq and met with Saddam Hussein. He and his companions "got in there [into Iraq] supernaturally," surveyed the situation, and met with "more leaders than I think any-one in America has even thought about meeting with in the last couple of years." He seemed dazzled by the royal treatment he received: An assistant Iraqi ambassa dor met them and escorted them to Bagdad, and "we were really in style, we were riding across the desert in a nice Mercedes." They stayed in the guest house of the presidential palace, and "that wasn't bad at all."

Cain described meetings with various Iraqi officials and with Saddam Hussein himself. These meetings, he said, were "very cordial . . . we explained that we felt like God had shown us some of the injustices that had taken place." Iraqi officials told him in graphic detail of the casualties and sufferings Iraq has endured because of the war and the sanctions imposed afterward. While Cain did not say Iraq is without blame for the conflict, he seemed to place most of the blame on the United States. He contrasted the Desert Storm operation with our intervention in "Somalia, wherever that place is; we didn't start the trouble there, but we did start the trouble here [in Iraq]; it's one thing for people to be dying, and us do nothing about it, but it's another thing for us to be the cause of those people dying."

Cain said that his meeting with Saddam began with the usual greetings, and then "I started the meeting with President Saddam Hussein by repenting on the part of America for what we've done to that nation, to him, and to his people." Saddam was deeply moved by this repentance, according to Cain, and said some very moving things in return. Saddam is a powerful military leader, Cain told the group, but "he is not a madman; all of Iraq seems to love him." Saddam asked what America, "the last of the great superpowers," and President Bush had to gain from invading Iraq, apparently never mentioning Iraq's invasion and seizure of Kuwait and the atrocities committed there. Cain told Saddam that "President Clinton is the hope of America right now," and Saddam responded that "President Clinton is not only the hope of America, he's the hope of Iraq and he's the hope of the whole world." Saddam told Cain that he had tried to solve problems by force, but "what ultimately brought peace was when God gave him wisdom, Almighty God gave him wisdom to go and sit down with his enemies and to reason with them." Was Saddam speaking of the same God Paul Cain worships? The question does not seem to have even occurred to Cain. They toured the country, and when they parted Cain was told, "You are welcome in Iraq at any time."

The American media have not told the truth about Iraq, Cain said in his Abundant Life Speech, and they have "demonized" Saddam Hussein. Cain said that when America and the United Nations "destroyed" Iraq, "we were working directly against the purposes of Almighty God and His Christ." He believes, however, that U.S. officials who willfully deceived the American people will be exposed and will have a "dark place alongside the likes of Hitler and men like that."

It is, of course, possible that we haven't been given the full story, and that there is another side to the Iraqi conflict that Americans haven't been told. But did Paul Cain receive the true story? He's convinced Iraqi officials told him the truth: "I knew this man was telling me the truth, because I prayed for the Spirit of truth to be in operation."

However, one can't help comparing Cain's experience in Iraq to the red carpet treatment given liberal American religious leaders by Josef Stalin; they returned to the United States thoroughly convinced that Stalin was a benevolent father figure who was building a wonderful Socialist workers' paradise for his people and enjoyed their wholehearted love and support. Smart dictators know how to spot and manipulate such people and use them as propaganda fodder.

Could Cain's naivete about Saddam Hussein be reflected in his naivete about Clinton? Could Clinton and his aides have recognized in Paul Cain a well-meaning but naive religious figure who could be utilized to divide the Christian community and neutralize its opposition to the Clinton agenda? The possibility should not be ignored.

I will not pass judgment upon Paul Cain's sincerity or character. While the possibility of deception exists, I am not prepared to say whether or not Paul Cain is intentionally deceiving people about his "vision" from the Lord. But his track record indicates an overemphasis on personal revelation independent of the Bible, and possible doctrinal error. Given this record, the factual discrepancies concerning the fulfillment of the prophecy, and the circumstances under which the "vision" was transmitted and received, it is difficult to give the vision much credibility.

Does God speak through dreams and visions today? Christians are divided on that question. Without doubt He spoke through dreams and visions before the Canon of Scripture was completed. Now that the Bible is available in finished form, many believe, God speaks only through His Word and not through extrabiblical revelation because God knows that a written standard is necessary so man can distinguish true revelation from the counterfeit.

Other Christians believe God continues to speak through dreams and visions today, using these devices to communicate and illuminate truths already found in the Bible or to show people how to apply those truths, but that He does not communicate new truths not already found in His Word. Christians can disagree on this question, but this difference of opinion need not affect our evaluation of Paul Cain's vision.

Whichever view one takes, I do not believe Paul Cain has correctly interpreted the will of God. In reaching this conclusion, I do not pass judgment upon Paul Cain's sincerity or his character. I would like to believe that Paul Cain is a likable and well-meaning Christian who is simply naive and impressionable and perhaps prone to confuse his own feelings and ideas with the will of God, and who is therefore being deceived and manipulated by forces (human or spiritual) that he doesn't really understand.

However, his propensity for extrabiblical revelation, his willingness to endorse and associate with "prophets" who teach heresy, the possible alternate explanations for his knowledge of the headlines, the discrepancy in his reporting of the headlines, the fact that the Clinton administration thus far shows no signs of moving in the directions Paul Cain predicted, and the subsequent actions of Paul Cain in Iraq lead me to conclude that Paul Cain does not speak for the Lord in this matter.

Having reached this conclusion, I must further conclude that the effect of Paul Cain's vision upon those who believe it is the division of Christians, the neutralization of their effectiveness in combating the antibiblical policies of the Clinton administration, and the prevention of their working for pro-life, pro-family, and other biblically based policies. The long-term effect of this vision, then, is to prevent Christians from being salt of the earth and light unto the world.

chapter 2

Bill and Hillary Clinton: Politically Correct or Biblically Correct?

Paul Cain writes, "The Lord loves and intends to use Bill Clinton. The Lord does not see him as he is, but as the man he will become" (*Morning Star Prophetic Bulletin*, January 1993, p. 2).

We do not know what kind of man Bill Clinton will become. But we can ask, what kind of man is Bill Clinton? And how did he become the man he is? I plan to focus, not upon what Bill Clinton has done, but upon what Bill Clinton believes. What are his ultimate values, and how were they formed? What does he plan to do as president, and how will he achieve those goals?

Is Bill Clinton a Christian? Some say he is; others vigorously deny it. I cannot answer that question definitively and will not even try.

Let us remember this and keep it in perspective: A Christian is a sinner who acknowledges his sin and trusts the Lord Jesus Christ and His finished work on the Cross for his salvation. In this sense, whether Bill Clinton is a Christian in his heart of hearts is a question only he and the Lord can answer.

Of far greater importance—not for the sake of getting into heaven, but for the purpose of running the country—is whether Bill Clinton's viewpoint on the fundamental issues facing America today is consistent with the principles and values found in the Word of God.

People of different persuasions often find themselves talking past one another on points like this, not really understanding what the other is saying. I recall a faculty meeting at a Christian university some years ago, at which one professor said abortion was contrary to the Bible. Another professor took offense, calling the first professor narrow and judgmental.

As they argued, it became apparent to me that the two professors—both believing evangelical Christians— weren't really hearing one another, and were virtually talking different languages.

The first professor was saying, "Abortion isn't biblical." The second was thinking, "He's saying I'm not a Christian because I believe in legalized abortion."

In fact, that's not what the first professor was saying at all—though perhaps he could have articulated his point more clearly. He had said that the Bible teaches against abortion. He did not mean to imply that one who holds a different view about abortion cannot be a Christian. He meant that the second professor had misinterpreted the Bible on that point, but he did not mean that a correct understanding of the biblical teaching on that point was a litmus test of Christianity. One becomes a Christian by believing in Jesus Christ. One can believe in Jesus Christ and be mistaken about abortion, and one can be biblically correct on abortion without believing in Jesus Christ.

Conservatives and liberals commonly talk past one another like this. In 1988, Democratic presidential candidate Michael Dukakis was accused of being "anti-family." He responded that the charge was completely untrue, that he was a good husband and father. But that was not the issue. The issue was not Michael Dukakis's family life; the issue was whether the national policies Candidate Dukakis advocated—subsidized day care, etc.—were harmful to families. One might be a very good parent but advocate policies that undermine the family unit, perhaps without realizing that these policies could have that effect.

On another occasion I represented a school board in a controversy involving Bible studies in the public schools. The American Civil Liberties Union had demanded that the Bible studies cease. Most of the audience at the public meeting of the board wanted the board to retain the Bible study and fight the ACLU. A few wanted the board to accede to the ACLU's demands, citing the costs of the lawsuit as their primary reasons.

Supporters of the Bible study stressed the beneficial effects of the Bible study upon the children of the community and the unfairness of depriving the children of this study. Opponents kept repeating that they themselves prayed at home and church and that "we're God-fearing people." That may have been true, but it wasn't the issue. The issue was the constitutionality of the Bible study and its beneficial effects upon the children and the community; the personal religious practices of the opponents (or supporters) were irrelevant. It would have been equally inappropriate for supporters to make an issue of their own personal piety or their opponents' lack thereof, but in this instance they did not do so.

This often happens in discussions of national policy. Conservatives, especially conservative Christians, stress the need for values in public life. Liberals, often misinterpreting "separation of church and state" to mean that values have no place in public life, often retreat to their personal lives and values, and misinterpret criticism of their public positions as attacks upon their personal character. (Conservatives, for their part, often fail to make that distinction clear.)

The question is not whether a candidate or public official holds values. The question is, what values? The fact is, everyone holds certain values. Some hold sound values; others hold values that are mistaken, distorted or warped. Even a thief holds values; in his warped value system, his personal gain is of greater importance than the property rights of others. And ultimately one's value system is rooted in one's religious beliefs—what one believes about God, man, the nature of God and man, what God has done for man, what God expects of man, etc. For that reason a culture built by Christians will have a different flavor and value system than a culture built by Muslims, or Hindus, or New Age pagans, or secularists.

It is a mistake, therefore, to say that society cannot legislate morality. For all law, all public policy, has a moral basis. That moral basis is grounded in ultimate values, and these values have their roots in religion.

Our laws against murder reflect the Ten Commandments, and they further reflect the Judeo-Christian belief that man is created in the image of God and that human life is therefore of infinite value. We also punish cruelty to animals, but not as severely as cruelty to people, because in our Judeo-Christian value system people are of greater importance than animals. Many in various forms of New Age earth-worship believe differently. Believing that animals are of equal value with people, they would increase the penalties for hurting animals; some would punish the killing of an unborn eagle but not the killing of an unborn human. That's a value judgment!

Property laws also involve value judgments. We punish theft because we recognize property rights. We make moral decisions as to who is entitled to own what property, and we enact those moral decisions into law and enforce them against those whose value systems are otherwise.

Even taxation involves moral judgments as to who should pay for what services. If we decide to finance public projects with "sin taxes" on products like alcohol and tobacco, we are making value judgments and enacting them into law. If we were to adopt an income tax by which the poor pay 90 percent and the rich pay only 10 percent, that would be denounced as immoral. The point is, even taxation involves value judgments that society has chosen to enact into law.

The question, then, is not whether the public positions of Bill and Hillary Clinton are rooted in values. Clearly they are. The question is, what values? Are the values of Bill and Hillary Clinton consistent with the traditional values held by most Americans and found in the Bible?

This chapter will focus upon what Bill and Hillary Clinton believe. It will not address their personal lives except insofar as their personal lives help us understand their beliefs.

So who are Bill and Hillary Clinton? Where did they come from, and how did they become the persons they are today?

The Making of Bill Clinton

In November 1945, Bill and Virginia Blythe conceived a child. Several months later, Bill found a job in Chicago and planned to raise his family there.

But it was not to be. In spring 1946, while driving

back to Hope, Arkansas, to bring Virginia and their unborn child to Chicago, Bill was killed in a car accident. The child he never saw, William Jefferson Blythe IV, was born four months later, on August 19.

During his early childhood years, Bill Blythe IV was raised partly by his mother and partly by his grandparents while his mother studied to be a nurse anesthetist. His family could be called working class, not wealthy but not destitute either.

In 1950, when Bill was four, his mother married Roger Clinton, and eventually Bill took his stepfather's name. Six years later Bill's stepbrother, Roger Clinton, was born. The younger Roger is now a singer and songwriter, and works as a production assistant for the sitcom "Designing Women." The elder Roger Clinton was, among other things, a Buick dealer. His problems with alcoholism and domestic violence made the Clinton home unstable at times, but despite this Bill and his stepfather seem to have genuinely cared for one another.

Bill Clinton spent most of his childhood in the public schools, though he attended a Catholic school for second grade as a transition between the Hope, Arkansas, schools and the Hot Springs schools. Even though his family was Baptist, he chose a Jesuit-run Catholic university, Georgetown, for his undergraduate college education. There he was elected freshman class president and was defeated for student council president several years later (One can imagine the victor, Terry Mogdlin, now knowing that he once defeated the man who later became president of the United States!).

But Clinton's interest went beyond student government; national politics fascinated him at least from 1956, when he watched the Democratic vice-presidential contest between John F. Kennedy and Estes Kefauver on his family's new black-and-white television. Four years later Kennedy remained his idol: "I decided to be a Democrat starting in the presidential election of 1960," he later wrote, "when John Kennedy excited me with a promise to get the country moving again."

Liberal politicians and liberal causes continued to surround Bill Clinton. In 1963, as a high school junior, he attended Boys' Nation, met President Kennedy, and had lunch in the Senate Dining Room with Arkansas Sen. J. William Fulbright, a leading liberal and outspoken critic of anti-Communist foreign policy.

Senator Fulbright apparently made a lasting impression on Clinton. Two years later, as a freshman at Georgetown in Washington, D.C., Clinton became an administrative and research assistant for Fulbright, who was then Chairman of the Senate Foreign Relations Committee. Fulbright's early and outspoken opposition to American involvement in Vietnam undoubtedly affected Bill Clinton's own opposition to the war and refusal to serve in the armed forces. The School of Foreign Service at Georgetown likewise helped to shape his liberal philosophy of government.

In the fall of 1968, having graduated from Georgetown the previous spring, Clinton went as a Rhodes Scholar to Oxford in England, where he organized an international protest against America's war to contain communism in Southeast Asia. Having avoided the draft by an ROTC deferment, he subsequently gave up his ROTC deferment and subjected himself to the draft—but only two days after the 1969 draft lottery had occurred and Clinton's number (311) virtually assured him that he would not be called up. When, at Oxford, a friend named Frank Aller received a draft notice and decided to refuse to serve, a party in his honor was thrown in Bill Clinton's room.

Now safe from military service, Clinton returned to the United States in summer 1970 and enrolled in Yale Law School. The first semester he worked in the senatorial campaign of anti-war candidate Joe Duffy, serving as his campaign manager for the Third District.

And there he met a young lady named Hillary Rodham.

Enter Hillary

While every First Lady has been influential, few have held the power of Hillary Rodham Clinton. The *New York Times* described her as "the dominant figure in the election" (18 May 1992). *Newsweek* called her "a driving force in her husband's political career. . . . The dominant personality in the race" (30 March 1992). *Vanity Fair* called her "the diesel engine powering the front-running Democratic campaign" (June 1992).

"Who Elected *Her*?" a bumper sticker asks. The fact is that while Hillary's name did not appear on the ticket, she made clear from the beginning that she plans to take an active role in the White House. "I expect to be involved in helping to bring about changes in those areas in which I have an abiding interest," she told *Newsweek* 30 March 1992. And on 3 April 1992 she told "CBS This Morning," "If you vote for my husband, you get me; it's a two-for-one, blue plate special." A portrait of President Clinton would therefore be incomplete without looking at the First Lady.

Hillary Rodham was born on October 26, 1947, in Chicago—ironically, where Bill might have been born and raised had his father not died four months before he was born.

But there the background similarities end. Unlike Bill's working-class background, his mother's second marriage and his stepfather's bouts with alcoholism and domestic violence, Hillary's family were stable, upper-middle-class Chicago suburbanites—and like most stable, upper-middle-class Chicago suburbanites, staunch conservative Republicans. In fact, in 1964 at age 16 Hillary went door to door campaigning for Goldwater! Entering Wellesley College in 1965, she became president of the College Republicans.

But even before this time, forces of change were at work within Hillary. One major influence was Don Jones, then youth minister at the Rodhams' First Methodist Church. Jones had studied under theologian Paul Tillich at Drew University, and as Hillary told *Newsweek*, "He was just relentless in telling us that to be a Christian did not just mean you were concerned about your own personal salvation." Jones took Hillary and the other youths on trips to the inner city, had them meet with black gangs, organized babysitting for the children of migrant workers, and introduced them to current art, literature, and culture. Through Don Jones, Hillary heard and met Dr. Martin Luther King, Jr., and she frequently stopped by Jones's office to talk after school. As Jones says, "She was intellectual even then. She was open-minded. She was curious, open to what life had to bring. When I introduced her to a lot of new things, she was just insatiable." Among other things, Jones introduced her to the writings of Tillich, Bonhoefer, Reinhold Niebuhr, and J. D. Salinger.

As a college political science major, Hillary was ready for change. Her primary influence in college seems to have been Professor Alan Schechter, a staunch liberal. Under his tutelage Hillary quickly moved from her conservative roots through the liberal wing of the Republican Party, and soon beyond the GOP. By 1968 she was campaigning for ultra-liberal Democratic presidential candidate Eugene McCarthy, and later for Hubert Humphrey, and had adopted granny dresses and horned-rim glasses. She wrote her senior thesis on community action programs for the poor, arguing that longer term programs were necessary to achieve lasting impact.

After Wellesley she went to Yale Law School, where she met Bill Clinton. While at Yale she worked for a public interest civil rights group called the Washington Research Project, raising her own funds by tapping a law school research grant. Among other tasks, her work for the Washington Research Project put her in touch with Sen. Walter Mondale, whose senate subcommittee was studying the conditions of workers in migrant labor

camps. She then began working for Yale's Child Study
Center and later the Carnegie Council on Children; she
also developed programs for children at Yale's Legal
Services Organization.

The Bill and Hillary Team

In the summer of 1972 Bill and Hillary worked
together in Texas, Bill heading George McGovern's
campaign office in Austin, Hillary registering Hispanic
voters for the Democratic National Committee.

After graduation in 1973, Hillary served as a staff
attorney for the Children's Defense Fund, and then
worked for the special counsel on the House Judiciary
Committee researching issues concerning the pending
impeachment of President Nixon.

Unlike Hillary, Bill felt a deep attachment to his
home state and was determined to return to Arkansas.
He took a position teaching at the University of Arkansas Law School in Fayetteville in 1973, and the following
year he ran for Congress in northwest Arkansas's Third
District, losing to Congressman John Hammerschmidt
in a close race.

Hillary's work on the House Judiciary Committee
came to an end in 1974 with Nixon's resignation. She
could have had many opportunities in places like Washington, D.C., but she chose instead to come to Arkansas, working in Bill's unsuccessful congressional campaign. She then secured a position at the University of
Arksansas Law School in Fayetteville and taught with
Bill. They were married on 11 October 1975.

Their careers continued to blossom. Bill was elected
Arkansas attorney general in 1976, and governor in
1978. Hillary, meanwhile, became a partner in the pres-
tigious Rose Law Firm and also served on the Board of
Directors of the Washington-based Legal Services Cor-
poration and helped found Arkansas Advocates for Children.

Two years later in 1980, Bill Clinton's career received a severe setback when he was defeated for reelection by evangelical Christian businessman Frank White. Observers attributed the defeat to a number of factors: problems during Clinton's first term of office; overreliance upon out-of-state advisors making Clinton seem arrogant and out of touch with Arkansas; alienation of various voting blocs and interest groups; various Carter policies; the Reagan victory nationwide. In the view of some, however, Hillary had contributed to Bill's defeat by refusing to be a traditional governor's wife. There were those who believed her hippie-style dress, career independence and refusal to take her husband's last name may have cost the support of some tradition-minded Arkansas voters.

In fact, one may draw certain parallels between Clinton's first term as governor of Arkansas and the first months of his presidency: a tax increase (car licenses in Arkansas), problems with health care reform, the Hillary factor. As governor, Clinton had appointed Hillary chairman of a forty-four member state Rural Health Advisory Committee; as president he placed Hillary in charge of national health reform.

The reelection defeat was hard to swallow. At age 34 Bill Clinton suddenly found himself the nation's youngest ex-governor, and it seemed as though his career was finished. As Judith Warner writes,

> Clinton, faced with his loss, wept openly. Election night he withdrew unto himself, leaving Hillary to deal with reporters and well-wishers and to extend gracious words to the incoming Whites. (Judith Warner, *Hillary Clinton: The Inside Story* [New York: Signet, 1993], p. 107)

But eventually Bill Clinton bounced back from his loss and resolved to make a political comeback. Admitting he had made some mistakes, he announced for governor again in 1982. Hillary campaigned at his side, this time restyled as Hillary Clinton, not Hillary Rodham. In November the voters placed Bill Clinton back in the office he continued to hold until he became president in 1993.

The picture that emerges of Bill and Hillary Clinton, then, is of two people who are firmly rooted in liberal philosophies, liberal politicians, liberal organizations, and liberal solutions to the nation's problems. Some say Clinton is a new type of Democrat, not a traditional liberal. His past associations and past causes would indicate that he is every bit as liberal as previous Democratic presidential candidates—George McGovern, Walter Mondale, Michael Dukakis. Unlike those candidates, Clinton learned, at least after his 1980 defeat, that he could not win as a Kennedy-type liberal, certainly not in Arkansas, and probably not in the nation. Utilizing his folksy down-home manner and capitalizing upon the common misconception that there are no liberals in the South, Clinton has been able to package himself as something new and different. But the Clintons' platforms and programs speak for themselves, as do those of the 1992 Democratic National Platform upon which they ran.

Politically Correct vs. Biblically Correct

It is not possible, in this brief space, to fully articulate a biblical view of the various issues confronting Americans today. I have attempted to do this in some detail in *God and Caesar: Christian Faith and Political Action* (Wheaton: Crossway, 1984, 1992).

But it is important to compare the Clinton agenda to biblical principles of government. So let us look briefly at several key issues:

The Family

Humans cannot function without leadership, and the basic unit of authority in human society is the family. Through the family God has arranged for children to be born, their material and emotional needs supplied (1 Tim. 5:8; Matt. 7:9-11), and their instructional needs fulfilled (1 Cor. 14:35; Eph. 6:4; Prov. 4:1-2, 10-11; Deut. 6:5-7; 11:18-21). To strengthen the family unit, God's Word commands children to obey their parents (Exod. 20:12; Eph. 6:1; Col. 3:20).

Those who would honor these principles would therefore take a dim view of government intervention in the family unit or government policies that weaken the family unit. Yet the Clinton administration proposes to repeal the Young Child Tax Credit, despite campaign promises to increase it. To help families, Clinton has secured passage of the mandatory Family Leave Act by which employers are required to give leave to fathers and mothers of newborn children. One could argue that this helps families; however, the act requires employers to provide this benefit even though the employee might choose a different benefit, such as life insurance or increased health care, instead. And the mandatory leave act, combined with the repeal of the Young Child Tax Credit, has the net effect of discriminating against the stay-at-home parent who loses the tax credit but doesn't benefit from leave from work.

The Clinton agenda would further weaken families by renewing the "marriage penalty" which had been corrected by President Reagan's Tax Reform Act of 1986. Under President Clinton's proposed tax package, two lovers who live together unmarried would each pay $5,425 less in federal income taxes than they would pay if they were married to each other.

The pro-family position does not mean children have no rights, or that they are the property of their parents. Children are human beings created in the image of

God, and as such they are endowed with God-given rights. But because of their age and immaturity they are not capable of exercising their rights and making decisions for themselves. God in His wisdom has therefore placed them in the care of parents, who know them and love them more than anyone else and make decisions in their best interest.

Hillary Clinton, however, has made it clear that she rejects this view:

> I want to be a voice for America's children . . . advocating . . . the immediate abolition of the legal status of minority and the reversal of the legal presumption of the incompetence of minors in favor of a presumption of competence; the extension to children of all procedural rights guaranteed to adults; the rejection of the legal presumption of the identity of interests between parents and their children, and permission for competent children to assert those independent interests in the courts. (*Harvard Educational Review*, 1974)

On another occasion she wrote in the *Harvard Educational Review* (1973),

> If the law were to abolish the status of minority and to reverse its assumption of children's incompetency, the result would be an implicit presumption that children, like other persons, are capable of exercising rights and assuming responsibilities until it is proven otherwise. Empirical differences among children would then serve as the grounds for making exceptions to this presumption and for justifying rational state restrictions.

Her statements go beyond "kiddie-lib" and attack the very institution of marriage itself. She compares marriage to slavery:

The basic rationale for depriving people of rights in a dependency relationship is that certain individuals are incapable or undeserving of the right to take care of themselves and consequently need social institutions specifically designed to safeguard their position. Along with the family, past and present, examples of such arrangements include marriage, slavery, and the Indian reservation system. (1982, quoted in *American Spectator,* August 1992)

Or, as she said in *Public Welfare* (Winter 1978):

Certain myths . . . serve only to inhibit the development of a realistic family policy in this country: the myth of the housewife whose life centers only on her home and . . . the myth, or perhaps more accurately, the prejudice, that each family should be self-sufficient.

As the governor's wife, Hillary declined the traditional housewife model for herself, saying brusquely, "I suppose I could have stayed at home and baked cookies and had teas" (*New York Times,* 17 March 1992).

Hillary Rodham Clinton's personal lifestyle is her choice, based upon her own value system. But when her values become reflected in national policies that affect all Americans, including millions of American women who have chosen to be full-time homemakers and mothers, it becomes appropriate to inquire whether these values are more politically correct than biblically correct.

Gay Rights

As the Clinton presidency began, few issues were more explosive than his proposal to lift the ban on homosexuals serving in the armed forces. This proposal caused a national furor in which millions of Americans were galvanized into action. As a result, the attempt to lift the ban by executive order was placed on hold, and as of this writing the outcome is uncertain.

Americans should not have been surprised by the president's proposal. The 1992 Democratic National Platform called for "civil rights protection for gay men and lesbians and an end to Defense Department discrimination." Orders allowing the hiring of homosexuals in other federal departments are already being implemented, and a substantial number of actual or suspected homosexuals and/or gay rights advocates have been appointed to high-level federal positions.

It seems certain that the issue will not go away in July, regardless of what kind of executive order is issued. For the question of gays in the military is really a small portion of a much larger question—the role of homosexuals in society as a whole.

As of this writing, proposals for compromise are in the works. Sen. Sam Nunn (D-GA), Chairman of the Senate Armed Services Committee, has proposed a "Don't ask, don't tell" compromise under which new recruits would not be asked their sexual orientation, but if they reveal it while on duty they will be subject to discharge. Congressman Barney Frank (D-MASS) has proposed a further compromise under which, in addition to the "Don't ask, don't tell" proposal, military authorities will not investigate reports of homosexual activity engaged in by military personnel off post. In my judgment these compromises are unworkable for at least two reasons: (1) We would be admitting into the armed forces personnel who have a propensity for engaging in acts which we say we will not allow. These personnel will soon demand the right to engage in homosexual conduct the same as others can engage in heterosexual conduct. To allow such people to enter the armed forces is merely asking for trouble in the very near future. This proposal, in my opinion, is nothing but a halfway house to full acceptance of homosexual conduct. (2) Congressman Frank's "don't investigate" proposal breaks down a basic cornerstone of military discipline: the concept that a soldier is on duty twenty-four hours per day and that his actions affect the mission and image of the armed forces whether on or off duty, on or off post, in or out of uniform.

The homosexual drive for public acceptance is predicated upon the assumption that homosexuality is "normal." The linchpin of this argument is the oft-quoted but much-inflated Kinsey statistic that homosexuals constitute 10 percent of the population. In my recent book, *Gays & Guns: The Case Against Homosexuals in the Military* (Lafayette, LA: Huntington House, 1993), I dispute this figure, pointing out that Kinsey's 10 percent figure pertains only to male adults who were almost exclusively homosexual for at least three years during their adult lifetimes, and that Kinsey's figures are inflated because he used only volunteers, including those who attended his sex seminars and prisoners at penal institutions. I argued in the book that homosexuals actually constitute 2 percent of the population or less, citing several studies that support that conclusion.

Since the book went to press, a new study indicates that my 2 percent figure may have been, if anything, high. Published in the March-April 1993 issue of *Family Planning Perspectives*, the magazine of the Alan Guttmacher Institute, the study by the Battelle Human Affairs Research Center found that just 2.3 percent of men reported any homosexual activity in the past ten years and only 1.1 percent reported exclusively homosexual sex.

Despite the extremely small percentage of the population that is homosexual, according to the Center for Disease Control 67 percent of all AIDS cases are directly attributable to homosexual activity. Other studies demonstrate that homosexuals are disproportionately at risk of acquiring many other diseases, such as Hepatitis A, B, and C, syphilis, gonorrhea, rectal cancer, and many others. Three factors account for this disproportionate risk: (1) the fact that practicing homosexuals have many times more sexual partners during their lifetimes than do heterosexuals; (2) the fact that large percentages of homosexuals engage in practices like anal sex and analingual (anal/oral) sex that place them in contact with excrement and bodily fluids; (3) the propensity of homosexuals to engage in drug and alcohol abuse (about three times the national average).

Is there a basis for saying homosexuality is abnormal? I believe there is: (1) the ancient and modern moral proscriptions against such conduct, not only in Judeo-Christian societies but others as well; (2) the fact that homosexuals constitute such a small percentage of the population (1-2 percent rather than 10 percent); (3) the vile and offensive nature of many homosexual practices (I think it would be difficult for homosexuals to tell the public that practices such as urination and defecation on partners and tongue-in-anus sex are "normal" behavior); (4) the harmful health consequences of homosexual conduct, both for the individual and for others; and (5) the close association of homosexuality with other problems such as suicide, emotional disorders such as anxiety and depression, and drug and alcohol abuse.

The other cornerstone of the homosexual drive for public acceptance is the myth that people are "born" homosexual and are unable to change. If that is true, they argue, they should not suffer discrimination for something that is not their fault. Since it is so central to their position, they argue the point passionately.

The evidence strongly indicates that homosexuality is not an inborn characteristic. The testimony of many homosexuals who have left that lifestyle, the fact even according to Kinsey that large numbers drift in and out of homosexuality, the assurance of Masters and Johnson that the cure rate of homosexuals in therapy (if they desire to change) is very high, and the help of Christian support groups like Exodus International, all demonstrate that homosexuality is a lifestyle one chooses, not an inborn characteristic.

The third linchpin of the homosexual drive for public acceptance is the concept that homosexuals don't bother anyone else. The fact is, about one-third of all cases of pedophilia or child sex abuse involve homosexuals. While many homosexuals, possibly a majority, do not attempt to seduce "straight" people, some do. The gentlemanly bearing of some gay former military personnel stands in marked contrast to the conduct of those involved in the 25 April 1993 Gay March on Washington, where homosexuals marched undressed, performed sex acts in the presence of children, and engaged in speeches and chants with foul language. One group of thousands filed past the White House chanting, "Chelsea! Chelsea!"; another chanted, "10 percent is not enough! Recruit! Recruit! Recruit!"

An article by Michael Swift that appeared in the *Gay Community News* of 15-21 February 1987 may not speak for a majority of homosexuals but is chilling nevertheless:

> We shall sodomize your sons. . . . We shall seduce them in your schools, in your dormitories, in your gymnasiums, in your locker rooms, in your sports arenas, in your seminaries, in your youth groups, in your movie theater bathrooms, in your army bunk-houses, in your truck stops, in your all-male clubs, in your houses of Congress, wherever men are with men together. Your sons shall become our minions and do our bidding. They will be recast in our image. They will come to crave and adore us.
>
> We are everywhere, we have infiltrated your ranks. Be careful when you speak of homosexuals because we are always among you; we may be sitting across the desk from you; we may be sleeping in the same bed with you.

The family unit will be abolished. . . . Perfect boys will be conceived and grown in the genetic laboratory.

. . . All churches who condemn us will be closed. Our only gods are handsome young men. . . . [reprinted in Congressional Record, 27 July 1987, E-3081]

In the face of this assault, we need to hold up the timeless standard of God's Word: "Thou shalt not lie with mankind, as with womankind; it is abomination" (Lev. 18:22). The prohibition is repeated across thousands of years in Old Testament and New Testament passages alike: Genesis 9:19-29, 19:19-29; Deuteronomy 23:17; Romans 1:26-27; 1 Corinthians 6:9-10; 1 Timothy 1:9-10. One need not adopt an overly strict or narrow biblical hermeneutic to understand that homosexuality is not God's plan for the human race.

God hates homosexuality, but He loves homosexuals. Christ died for the sins of the homosexual just as He died for the sins of the rest of us. And deliverance from this lifestyle, or deathstyle, is available through Jesus Christ and through good professional help. But He also said, "If ye love me, keep my commandments" (John 14:15), and He told the harlot, "Go, and sin no more" (John 8:11).

Policies that encourage public acceptance of that which God says is abomination and which experience shows is harmful, are not consistent with biblical principles of government.

Military Policy

God's Word does not teach pacifism; in fact, it teaches the opposite. Scripture teaches that just war is at times a legitimate exercise of national policy (Eccles. 3:8); that a strong defense deters aggression and helps to preserve peace (Luke 11:21-22; Neh. 4:7-18; Luke 14:31-32); and that refusing to fight for one's country can be a sin against God (Num. 32:1-23). War and military service are compatible with the words and character of our Lord Jesus Christ (John 2:15-16; Luke 22:36-38) and that of many great believers in the Old and New Testaments (Abraham, Moses, Caleb, Joshua, Gideon, David, Nehemiah, and the centurions of Matthew 8:5-13 and Acts 10-11). The Hebrew wording of the commandment "Thou shalt not kill" (Exod. 20:13) prohibits murder, not killing in war, and Jesus' admonition to "turn the other cheek" (Matt. 5:38-39) means we should not return insult for insult, not that we should refuse to defend our loved ones and our country against attack.

Thus far, Bill Clinton shows little evidence that he understands biblical principles of military policy. His own opposition to American efforts to contain Communist aggression in Southeast Asia, coupled with his own refusal to serve in the armed forces, do not indicate a fitness to serve as commander in chief of the armed forces.

His desire to trim the military budget is also a cause for concern. As we have seen, biblical principles call for a strong defense; but how much money is required for a "strong" defense? That might vary depending upon the external situation. With the current apparent dismantling of the Soviet empire, it may be possible to downscale the military somewhat from its needs of a decade ago. But Clinton's defense cuts go beyond those of the Bush administration and, in the opinion of many military experts, could leave our military forces unprepared and vulnerable.

Particularly, President Clinton's decision to stop the development of Strategic Defense Initiative (SDI) is inconsistent with his biblical duty as a civil ruler to keep his people safe from foreign attack.

Abortion

The Clinton administration stands squarely on the side of legalized abortion on demand, at taxpayers' expense, enforced by federal statute without regard to any state policies to the contrary. The 1992 Democratic National Platform states,

Democrats stand behind the right of every woman to
choose, consistent with Roe v. Wade, regardless of
ability to pay, and support a national law to protect
that right.

Note the clever language. The "right of every woman
to choose" *what*? "Consistent with Roe v. Wade" means
the right to end the life of her unborn child. "Regardless of ability to pay" means at taxpayers' expense (abortion clinics are not charitable institutions). "A national
law to protect that right" means a federal statute which
would prevent any states from passing laws protecting
the right to life.

Bill Clinton began his presidency with a determined
effort to implement these goals. Within a few days of
taking office, he signed an executive order implement-
ing abortions at military hospitals and allowing federal
employees to counsel women to have abortions. He is
actively promoting the so-called Freedom of Choice Act,
which would mandate abortion on demand for all states
through all nine months of pregnancy, regardless of
whether states want laws to the contrary. He is also
pressing for legislation to provide federal funding for
abortion, laws imposing special penalties for trespassing
at abortion clinics (unlike trespassing at other locations),
and regulations which would allow experimentation upon
live and dead unborn children. He has also promised
that his Supreme Court appointments will be pro-abortion.

The pro-abortion position is contrary to the principles found in the Bible. I believe the Bible clearly
teaches that the unborn child is a living human being.
Note, for example, that the biblical languages make no
distinction between born and unborn children (*brephos*
[baby], Luke 1:44, 2:12; 2 Tim. 3:15; *huios* [sons], Luke
1:31, 36; 3:22; *bne* [son], Gen. 25:21-24; 17:25; 9:19;
gehver [man], Job 3:3). Note, also, that the biblical authors identify themselves with the unborn child in the

womb (Ps. 139:13-16; Isa. 49:1; Jer. 1:5). Note, third, that the Bible speaks of the unborn child dying (Job 10:18-19; Jer. 20:15-18). Note, fourth, that the Bible affords legal protection to the unborn child (Exod. 21:22-25, in which the term "miscarriage" in some of the modern versions is simply a mistranslation of the Hebrew words *yehled* [fruit or child] and *yatsah* [depart or come out]). Note, fifth, that the Bible ascribes sin to the unborn child (Ps. 51:5); the fact that the child has a sinful nature from conception would indicate that the child is human from conception. And sixth, the unborn child shows signs of personhood (John the Baptist in Luke 1:44; Esau and Jacob in Gen. 25:22).

Even if one does not believe the unborn child is fully human until birth, this would not lead to the conclusion that abortion is justified. Abortion would still be a wrongful invitation to promiscuity and an interference with God's sovereign determination that a child should be born.

The Growth of Big Government

Israel started as a nation without a king, twelve tribes united in a loose confederation governed by judges. The twelve tribes practiced decentralized government, with local magistrates ruling over groups of ten, groups of fifty, groups of one hundred, and groups of one thousand (Exod. 18).

But in keeping with what appears to be a universal tendency in this fallen world, Israel gravitated toward an ever-stronger central government and an erosion of local and tribal authority. First the Israelites demanded a king, so they could be like the nations around them. Then, in the course of several generations, those kings gradually aggrandized power to themselves and became oppressive.

After the death of King Solomon, the people asked his son and successor Rehoboam to lighten their tax load. His older counselors urged him to accede to their requests, but his younger advisors told him to respond harshly. Rehoboam listened to the young hotheads and responded, "My father made your yoke heavy, and I will add to your yoke: my father also chastised you with whips, but I will chastise you with scorpions" (1 Kings 12:14). The result was the rebellion of Jeroboam and the ten northern tribes, and the splitting of the kingdom.

President Clinton proposes sweeping new federal programs: massive government involvement in education, law enforcement, health care, abortion funding, and other areas that properly belong to state and local government or to the private sector. The proposal to spend federal funds to add 100,000 new policemen to the fight against crime and drugs sounds laudable in some ways, but again, law enforcement is generally a state and local responsibility and a federally controlled police force could be a step toward federal tyranny. To finance these programs, Clinton proposes massive and oppressive new taxes.

In so doing, he is ignoring the advice of America's wise elder statesmen and is following the folly of Rehaboam—with predictable results.

The Clinton Appointments

Many of the president's programs will be carried out by his appointees. It is therefore appropriate to consider what types of people President Clinton has appointed to high-level positions. Many, though not all, of them reflect a far Left ideology and at times an anti-Christian agenda.

Consider a few:

* Donna Shalala, Secretary of Health and Human Services. Shalala had been chancellor of the University of Wisconsin at Madison from 1988 to 1993. According to *Heterodoxy* April 1992, during her tenure the academic reputation of the University of Wisconsin slipped, as she subordinated "every other aspect of life at the

University to the success of what she calls multiculturalism." The basic core curriculum at the university has been abolished, and students are now required to take a course with "an ethnic dimension" like Buddhist Theology or Hindu Mysticism in order to graduate. She replaced deans of the wrong color or gender with those who were more politically correct, and instituted strict "politically correct" speech codes on campus which were declared unconstitutional by a U.S. District Court.

An outspoken advocate of gay rights and abortion on demand, Shalala summed up her views of children and education in a speech at the University of Chicago on 15 November 1991, describing the upbringing of a hypothetical child named Renata in the year 2004:

> Renata doesn't know any moms who don't work, but she knows lots of moms who are single. She knows some children who only live with their dads, and children who have two dads, or live with their mothers and their grandmothers. In her school books there are lots of different kinds of friends and families.
>
> . . . At Thanksgiving time, Renata's teacher will tell a story about how people from Europe came to the United States, where the Indians lived. She will say, "It was just the same as if someone had come into your yard and taken all of your toys and told you they weren't yours anymore."

Emphasizing that Renata will "think of herself as being part of the world—not just her town or the United States," Shalala said we can bring this about by making it "our top priority in our communities and in our Congress."

* Johnetta Cole, Clinton transition team cluster co-ordinator for education, arts, labor, and the humanities. According to *Human Events* December 1992, Cole was active in the Communist front known as Venceremos

Brigade, running its affiliate, the Committee to Stop U.S. Aggression Against Cuba. *Human Events* also reported that according to documents found in the Grenada archives after the U.S. action in that country, "Cole was president of the U.S. Grenada Friendship Society, a front organization in support of the Communist dictatorship."

Cole was a professor at Hunter College in the early 1980s, while Donna Shalala was Hunter's president. She also belonged to the Soviet-controlled World Peace Council and its American affiliate, the U.S. Peace Council, which she helped found in 1979. She broke her affiliation with these groups in 1987, when with Shalala's help she became president of Spelman College. But she was listed in 1990 on the board of advisors of *Rethinking Marxism*, a journal the announced goal of which is to "discuss, elaborate and/or extend Marxian theory." She also acknowledges that she named one of her sons, Ethan Che Cole, in honor of Communist revolutionary Che Guevara.

* Janet Reno, Attorney General. According to "Newsscan" (vol 3, issue 5 May 1993),

> While Health and Human Services Secretary Donna Shalala was President of the University of Wisconsin, Florida attorney Jack Thompson was instrumental in opposing the sale of homosexual-advocacy audio tapes, which had been produced by the U of W, to the Dade County School System. Thompson charged that Shalala, who has been identified as a lesbian, influenced her friend, now-Attorney General Janet Reno, to start a disbarment proceeding against him. It proved such a farce that the Florida Bar Association was ultimately forced to pay Thompson a $20,000 settlement. Thompson also charged that the Judicial Qualifications Commission of the Florida Bar refused to recommend Reno for a federal judiciary because of her alleged homosexuality, some calling her a "pink beret." Before the Senate voted 98-0 to confirm

Janet Reno, one of the most poorly qualified Attorney Generals ever submitted for confirmation hearings, the nation was assured that the FBI had investigated Thompson's (and others') charges that Reno was a lesbian. Orrin Hatch called the charges "scurrilous." Thompson had given the FBI the names of several people who could confirm Reno's drunk driving and lesbian activities. He later contacted all those people, and not one had been contacted by the FBI. The FBI investigation which supposedly cleared Reno consisted of avoiding talking to those who had firsthand knowledge of her activities and could therefore claim the allegations were not substantiated. [American Freedom Movement, April 1993; *Christian News*, 29 March 1993]

* Dr. Joycelyn Elders, Director of the Arkansas Department of Health and Clinton nominee for Surgeon General of the United States. Matt Friedeman writes of her in the *Clarion-Ledger* (Jackson, MS, 31 March 1993):

She displays in her office an "Ozark Rubber Plant"—so called because yellow condoms hang from its stalks. Attached is a note: "Blooms mostly at night. Blooms vary in length, depending on owner. Blooms may wilt in chilly atmosphere." She wants to pour more money into a very expensive program that has proven itself an accelerator of both teenage pregnancy and abortions. She plans to institute explicit, no holds barred, sex education beginning with your kindergartner. She advises pro-lifers to "get over their love affair with the fetus" and charges they "love little children as long as they are in someone else's uterus." She derides the "celibate, male-dominated church, a male-dominated legislature, and a male-dominated medical profession." She promotes school-based health clinics in Arkansas to reduce the pregnancy rate, each one costing $100,000-$150,000 annually. If parents do not return a consent form to the school, the school assumes that the parent is giving consent, and medical decisions, including abortion, are made without parental knowledge. She is Dr. Joycelyn Elders, director of the Arkansas Department of Health, and Bill Clinton's choice for Surgeon General of the United States. "Governor," she has queried Clinton occasionally, "should I back off?" His typical response: "No, no, Joycelyn, I love it . . . keep it up." In fact, he has said, "I want you to do for the whole country what you've done for Arkansas."

* Roberta Achtenberg, Assistant Secretary of Housing and Urban Development. A militant lesbian, Achtenberg led the fight in San Francisco to cut off United Way funding for the Boy Scouts and bar them from using public facilities, because of the Scouts' refusal to admit homosexuals.

* Thomas Payzant, Assistant Secretary for Elementary and Secondary Education. As superintendent, Payzant expelled the Boy Scouts from the San Diego public schools because of their refusal to admit homosexuals.

* Les Aspin, Secretary of Defense. As a Democratic Congressman from Wisconsin, Aspin was a frequent and strident critic of the military. In recent years he may have mellowed somewhat, but he remains an advocate of deep defense spending cuts and of lifting the gay ban.

* Rather than face a difficult confirmation fight, President Clinton withdrew the nomination of Lani Guinier for the top civil rights post in the Justice Department because of her radical views. Among other things, Guinier had written in the *Michigan Law Review* (1991) that black political leaders are "authentic" only when they are "politically, psychologically, and culturally black"—in other words, they are not truly black leaders unless they share the radical liberal agenda. Withdrawing the nomination, President Clinton said he

had not read her writings, and if he had, he would not have nominated her. Yet he and Hillary had been classmates of Guinier at Yale Law School and had traveled halfway across the country to attend her wedding several years ago. It is appropriate to ask: If Clinton did not screen and approve her nomination, who did?

* Ruth Bader Ginsburg, Clinton's nominee for the Supreme Court. Having served as general counsel for the radical American Civil Liberties Union (1973-1980) and counsel for the ACLU Women's Rights Project (1972-1980), Ginsburg is firmly pro-abortion although she questions the rationale of *Roe v. Wade.* Ginsburg may have moderated somewhat since President Carter appointed her to the Circuit Court of Appeals in 1980; then again, her "moderation" may have been calculated to obtain a Supreme Court appointment. We may hope the Senate will give Ginsburg the same scrutiny that they gave Bork in 1987 and Thomas in 1991. We may pray, "God save this honorable Court—especially for the next four years!"

The Clintons and the Church

It would be unfair to say the Clintons are not religious people. Bill was raised as a Baptist, though he attended Catholic school for second grade and a Catholic undergraduate university, where he seems to have particularly enjoyed a course on comparative religion taught by the Jesuit Father Sebes. He retains his affiliation with the Baptist church today. In the ongoing battle between conservatives and moderates (read: liberals) in the Southern Baptist Convention, Clinton says he is "pretty much on the side of the moderates." He also claims to have an ecumenical frame of mind and occasionally goes to Pentecostal camp meetings. "I love those people because they live by what they say." He recently told *U.S. News & World Report,* "I really believe in a lot of the old-fashioned things like the constancy of sin, the possibility of forgiveness, the reality of redemption. . . . I pray virtually every day, usually at night, and I read the Bible every week."

On the other hand, some of his ideas sound like New Age philosophy: "I basically believe life is a continual search for real integrity, literally integration, trying to put your mind and your body and your spirit in the same place at the same time" (*Charisma,* October 1992, p. 28).

Raised a Methodist, Hillary was involved in church work as a teenager and seems to have developed some of her views on social involvement from her Methodist youth minister. She remains a Methodist, and she and Bill have attended separate churches during most of their married lives. Judith Warner writes in *Hillary Clinton: The Inside Story* (New York: Signet, 1993, p. 214)

> There came a point, when Chelsea was about ten, that for the sake of family unity, Hillary gave being a Baptist a try. She attended Bill's church and sent Chelsea to the Baptist Sunday school. But the experiment was short-lived. Though it was important to her that Chelsea freely choose her own church affiliation, and that the choice be as meaningful as Hillary's own confirmation into Methodism had been, she was nonetheless relieved when Chelsea chose Methodism. Dorothy Rodham [Hillary's mother] was glad too. She had been accused of blasphemy by Chelsea, who was then attending a Southern Baptist Sunday school, for saying, "Oh, my God," when she had accidentally knocked a glass off her kitchen counter. Some of the lay Sunday school teachers at Bill's church were extremely conservative. She didn't relish the idea of a fundamentalist Southern Baptist grandchild.

Within the last decade Hillary has become more regular in church attendance and has taught adult Sunday school classes and lectured about what it means to be a Methodist. According to Bishop Dick Wilke of the Arkansas area of the United Methodist Church,

> She understands the church beliefs biblically and theologically about as well as anybody I know. She's a Methodist by intellectual conviction. She's also done a great deal of study in the social positions of the Methodist Church, and I think she feels she's been guided in that direction. (Warner, p. 215)

Clearly the Clintons have some religious interest, but religious interest does not necessarily equate with real Christianity. Hillary talks about "crisis of meaning," social responsibility, and "defining yourself in your moment" (*Montgomery Advertiser*, 22 May 1993, C-1), but it is not clear what she means. Bill speaks about religious belief, but he shows little evidence that biblical values affect his public attitudes or public policies.

President Clinton's own denomination, the Southern Baptist Convention, at its 14-18 June 1993 annual meeting in Houston, passed a virtually unanimous resolution denouncing the president's policies on abortion and gay rights. The 17,000 delegates declared, "We as a convention, the denomination with which President Clinton has publicly identified, separate ourselves [from his policies] and urge him to affirm biblical morality in exercising his public office." They also asked fellow Baptists to "earnestly pray" for the president and to use their influence to try to convince him to "stand for biblical morality and to reverse his stands." Speaking at the Cooper Union School for the Advancement of Science and Art in New York early in 1993, President Clinton declared that

> We also have in this country a crisis of belief and hope. . . .
>
> This is a strange and, in a way, wondrous moment in our history, when citizens everywhere desperately want

things to change but still are wary of it and reluctant to place their faith in anyone's prescription. . . . If you don't remember anything else I say, I hope you'll remember this: The human condition in the end changes by faith. And faith cannot be held in your hand. The Scripture that I carry to my place of worship every Sunday says, "Faith is the assurance of things hoped for, the conviction of things unseen." But make no mistake about it, it is by far the most powerful force that can ever be mustered in the cause of change. (*Montgomery Advertiser*, 22 May 1993, C-1)

The question is: *Faith in what?*

chapter 3

Did God Vote for Bill Clinton?

Paul Cain and Rick Joyner declare in their *Morning Star Prophetic Bulletin* article,

Regardless of what we feel about his politics, Bill Clinton could not have been elected without God allowing it. Therefore, we must now ask ourselves, "Why did the Lord want Bill Clinton to be President and how should we respond to him?" (January 1993, p. 2)

Does anyone notice a leap of logic here? "Bill Clinton could not have been elected without God allowing it"— true enough. But then: "Why did the Lord want Bill Clinton to be President?" The logic runs: God *allowed*

Clinton to win, therefore God must have *wanted* Clinton to win. Does this necessarily follow?

One could, of course, apply the same reasoning to the rise to power of Hitler or Stalin. God allowed them to win; therefore He wanted them to win. In his lecture at Abundant Life Fellowship in Mt. Gilead, Ohio, Cain seemed to imply the same about Saddam Hussein; the fact that Saddam is still in power despite all of the efforts to remove him, indicates that God's hand is upon Saddam and somehow God plans to use him to accomplish His purposes in the Middle East. But does logic compel us to this conclusion?

Theologians commonly distinguish between the *directive* will of God and the *permissive* will of God. The directive will of God is that which God wills to happen and causes to happen. The permissive will of God is that which God does not necessarily want to happen, but allows to happen and often uses for His purposes.

For example, the persecution of Jews which took place in Europe during World War II certainly did not meet with God's approval. And yet, for reasons we cannot fully understand, God allowed it to happen. And through the experience many Jews came to eternal life through the knowledge of Jesus Christ, as through the ministry of people like Corrie ten Boom.

God hates sin, and He did not want sin to enter the world. But He allowed it to happen, and He allows each of us to be born with a sinful nature and to become sinners by nature and by choice. He also provides for us a Redeemer, His Son, the Lord Jesus Christ.

God loves all people, and He does not want anyone to reject Jesus Christ and lose eternal life: He is "not willing that any of these should perish, but that all should come to repentance" (2 Pet. 3:9). But He doesn't force people to repent and trust Jesus Christ; He allows people to choose to reject Christ. "Wide is the gate, and broad is the way, that leadeth to destruction, and many there be which go in thereat: Because strait is the gate, and narrow is the way, which leadeth unto life, and few there be that find it" (Matt. 7:13-14). He doesn't want anyone to perish, but He allows people to perish if they choose to reject Jesus Christ.

Suppose I want to fly to Denver for a speaking engagement, but God doesn't want me to go to Denver because He knows I need to stay home and finish writing my book. He may employ His directive will and prevent me from going to Denver, perhaps by sending a snowstorm to close the Denver airport. Or He may employ His permissive will and allow me to go to Denver, give the speech, and miss my book deadline. The former course of action might seem the more compassionate, sparing me the agony; but He might choose the latter because He knows I need a lesson on "How to say no."

Sometimes the directive and permissive wills of God are difficult to distinguish. For example, Leviticus 26:14-46 describes five cycles of discipline that are imposed upon a nation which turns away from God, each progressively more severe, beginning with loss of economic prosperity, escalating to violence and breakdown of law and order, then to military conquest and/or foreign occupation, and ultimately national destruction if the earlier cycles do not induce repentance. These cycles of discipline could be imposed by God's directive will, or He might simply allow the nation to reap the consequences of its own foolishness. The same is true of individuals. God may send disasters to turn us from our wrongful ways, or He may simply allow natural events to take their course: Crime leads to apprehension and imprisonment; spendthrift habits lead to financial ruin; drunkenness and gluttony lead to broken health.

In all of these forms of discipline, however, God's will is the same—that we should repent and return to fellowship with Jesus Christ. Discipline may be applied in various stages: warning discipline at first, then more intensive discipline, and finally dying discipline so that we may die in grace.

Some theologians add a third category of the will of God: His *overruling* will. Sometimes God allows people to pursue their evil ways, and then overrules their evil desires by using what they have done to achieve good. An example is found in Genesis, when Joseph's jealous brothers threw him into a pit and allowed him to be sold to the Egyptians as a slave. This was a sinful act, and God did not approve it. But He allowed it to happen, and He used it for His purposes. He caused Joseph to prosper in Egypt, eventually rising to become prime minister of Egypt, and through Joseph's wise economic and agricultural policies, Egypt had enough food stored to survive a seven-year famine and to feed Joseph's brothers as well. And when Joseph's brothers came down to Egypt to get food, and finally recognized Joseph as their brother, they repented of what they had done. But Joseph assured them, "Ye thought evil against me, but God meant it unto good" (Gen. 50:20).

Did God want Bill Clinton to become president? The Bible doesn't directly answer that question; looking under *C* in *Strong's Concordance*, Clinton's name is not mentioned. Considering the policies of the Clinton administration, it doesn't seem likely that God would favor a candidate who advocates such a program. The best man doesn't always win in politics—though occasionally the voters are more sensible and perceptive than we would like to admit.

Why, then, did God allow Bill Clinton to win the election? There might be several reasons:

(1) He may choose to discipline believers for their laxness and apathy. In the elections of 1980, 1984, 1988, and 1992, many Christians took their civic responsibilities seriously—but the majority did not. Except for voting, most Christians remained largely uninvolved in the election. Relatively few bothered to attend their precinct caucuses, express their views, or work actively for the candidates of their choice. And in 1992 the percentage of evangelicals who even bothered to vote dropped

to significantly less than the national average—and far less than the average turnout of homosexuals! If Christians had voted in the numbers they should have, they could have easily defeated Clinton. The Clinton administration therefore stands as a stark monument to remind Christians of the consequences of their apathy. The 1992 election was a race we didn't have to lose!

(2) God may have allowed the election of Bill Clinton to discipline the nation as a whole, or the nation's unbelievers.

Some say we live in post-Christian America. (While a large majority of Americans still identify themselves as Christians, many define that term in unorthodox ways.) Realistically, we must admit that the church in America today is a mere shadow of what it once was in terms of its influence upon American society, and that while large numbers of Americans still call themselves Christians, they often have little idea of what being a Christian is really all about.

It is therefore not surprising that post-Christian Americans would choose a president who reflects their post-Christian values. While Bill and Hillary Clinton may stand far to the Left of most Americans, few have the clear ideological foundation to say unequivocally that the Clinton agenda is wrong. So if they perceive Clinton as offering jobs or other economic benefits, no wonder the pocketbook wins out over shallow and ill-formed moral convictions.

We can understand, then, why Clinton won the election. But why did God allow the Clinton victory? Couldn't He have intervened?

Certainly He could have. We read in Daniel 2:21 that "He removeth kings, and setteth up kings." How He does this is a mystery. He probably doesn't cast a veto, or stuff the ballot box; more likely He causes or allows events to proceed in such a manner as to influence citizens to vote a certain way. But He can prevent an election victory if He chooses.

So why did God allow moral degeneracy to have its way in the last election? Possibly He intends through the Clinton agenda to teach Americans the folly of departing from their Judeo-Christian roots.

As a controlled, socialist economy degenerates into stagnation, Americans may realize that the free enterprise system is necessary to give people the incentive to produce.

As the nation drives God out of public life by forbidding prayer and Bible reading in public classrooms and graduation exercises, the nation experiences the consequences of forgetting God—i.e., schools filled with crime, drugs, and discipline problems, failure to teach moral values, and even failure to provide a good academic education.

As the nation closes down bases and then admits gays into the military and sees the consequent breakdown of discipline and morale, it may come to realize that the best weapons systems are of little value without trained, disciplined soldiers to man them.

As unprecedented taxes and regulations stifle the economy and cause American businesses to relocate abroad, Americans may come to realize that the original vision of the founding fathers was limited government, not big government.

As the nation moves toward tax-subsidized abortion and experiences the consequent cheapening of human life, Americans may realize the importance of the pro-life ethic.

In short, God may be using "shock therapy" on America—four years of the Clinton agenda to awaken Americans to their true values.

(3) God may have allowed the election of Bill Clinton because He knows that Clinton is going to change. God knows the future as He knows the past and present. It is possible that, despite the anti-biblical views Clinton holds today, he will change to a biblical ethic in the future. It is even possible that President Clinton will

find himself so overwhelmed with the swirling tide of national and international problems that beset the nation and the world, that he will realize the ideological bankruptcy of his advisors and their solutions, and he will turn to a biblical ethic as the ultimate solution.

Based on what we see and know today, this does not seem likely. But it is not beyond the realm of possibility. After all, who in A.D. 33 would have predicted the conversion of Saul of Tarsus? Or who in A.D. 380 would have predicted the conversion of Augustine? If Clinton were to change from his present position and become a champion of biblical values, this could be an example of the overruling will of God. The anti-Christian, pro-abortion, and pro-homosexual forces in society worked for Clinton's election and rejoiced at his victory. Most conservative Christians regarded his victory as a crushing defeat. If Clinton were to break with his current allies and embrace biblical values, it would be much like the brothers of Joseph: They meant it for evil, but God meant it for good. The liberal establishment brought about the election of Bill Clinton and thought it would advance their agenda, but God allowed them to win the election, then overruled them and caused the election to work for divine good.

I must emphasize, however, that I see no sign whatsoever, to date, that this is happening. There is no evidence that President Clinton has changed his liberal views in the least. We must be careful not to be caught up in idealism to the point where what we wish were happening is confused with what actually is happening.

A more likely way for the overruling will of God to work, in my opinion, is through strengthening the will of grassroots Americans. It is possible that four years of shock therapy, during which Americans see the radical policies of the Clinton administration, will awaken them to reality and cause them to understand that these policies are very foreign to their own values and that, furthermore, these policies are doomed to failure. After four years of disaster under Clinton, Americans may really be fed up and ready to return to their biblical roots. If so, in the long run the election of Bill Clinton could turn out to be a defeat for the radical Left and a victory for traditional values.

So, does the election of Bill Clinton reflect the directive will of God, the permissive will of God, or the overruling will of God? Based upon what we see and know so far, the permissive will of God is most likely. God didn't want Bill Clinton to win, but He permitted Bill Clinton to win to discipline Americans, shock them back to their senses, and bring them back to their biblical roots. While it is possible that Clinton could change in the future, he shows no sign of doing so, and therefore Christians cannot count on that possibility.

Whether the Clinton election reflects the directive, permissive, or overruling will of God, the role of Christians remains the same: to support and obey secular authority insofar as secular authority fulfills the divine function of government as set forth in Romans 13; to fervently oppose those policies of the Clinton administration that are contrary to biblical values; to pray for President Clinton and all who are in authority; to keep the door open for communication and cooperation with the Clinton administration in areas of common ground; and to learn the principles of civic government found in the Word of God so we don't let this mistake happen again!

Above all, in holding the door open for cooperation and communication we must not compromise our basic values. President Clinton is not likely to embrace biblical values if he sees Christians compromising on those values. We are much more likely to influence President Clinton by standing firm for what is right, than by accepting what is wrong.

chapter 4

Loyal Opposition: The Role of Loyalty

Would you support a president who is openly and notoriously anti-Christian?

- who was openly bisexual in his lifestyle?
- who was an unabashed idolator?
- who taxed his people heavily and used the tax revenues to promote his pagan religion?
- who presided over a very unfair and corrupt tax structure?
- who ran a Socialist welfare state?
- who persecuted Christians, subjecting them to all sorts of legal disabilities and even imprisonment, physical abuse, and death?

No? Then you would have had quite a problem supporting the Emperor Nero in ancient Rome.

Nero was all of the above and more. He was cruel, insane, and possibly demon-possessed. Christians were frequent victims in his gladiatorial games in the Coliseum, and he even wrapped Christians in oil-soaked rags, tied them to posts, set them afire, and used them as torches to light his garden parties.

And yet, the Apostle Paul told believers to be subject to the Emperor Nero.

He wrote in Romans 13:1-7:

> Let every soul be subject unto the higher powers. For there is no power but of God: the powers that be are ordained of God.
>
> Whosoever therefore resisteth the power, resisteth the ordinance of God: and they that resist shall receive to themselves damnation.
>
> For rulers are not a terror to good works, but to the evil. Wilt thou then not be afraid of the power? do that which is good, and thou shalt have praise of the same:
>
> For he is the minister of God to thee for good. But if thou do that which is evil, be afraid; for he beareth not the sword in vain: for he is the minister of God, a revenger to execute wrath upon him that doeth evil.
>
> Wherefore ye must needs be subject, not only for wrath, but also for conscience sake.
>
> For this cause pay ye tribute also: for they are God's ministers, attending continually upon this very thing.
>
> Render therefore to all their dues: tribute to whom tribute is due; custom to whom custom; fear to whom fear; honour to whom honour.

Think for a moment: Who was Paul's immediate audience? The answer is as obvious as who was buried in Grant's tomb: The epistle to the Romans was written to Romans, i.e., Christians living in the City of Rome.

And while the epistle to the Romans does not bear an exact copyright date, Bible scholars generally believe Paul wrote the epistle around A.D. 56. Nero reigned as Emperor of Rome from A.D. 54 to A.D. 68.

So when Paul told Roman Christians in A.D. 56 to be subject to the higher authorities, whom did he have in mind? More than one person perhaps, but above all others he clearly was referring to Nero!

Peter's exhortation is equally clear:

> Submit yourselves to every ordinance of man for the Lord's sake: whether it be to the king, as supreme,
>
> Or unto governors, as unto them that are sent by him for the punishment of evildoers, and for the praise of them that do well.
>
> For so is the will of God, that with well doing ye may put to silence the ignorance of foolish men:
>
> As free, and not using your liberty for a cloak of maliciousness, but as the servants of God.
>
> Honour all men. Love the brotherhood. Fear God. Honour the king. (1 Pet. 2:13-17)

Peter wrote this epistle around A.D. 65, again during the reign of Nero, and according to 1 Peter 1:1, his immediate audience were Christians scattered throughout the Roman Empire.

Peter tells us to submit to civil authorities from the highest to the lowest—from the emperor all the way down to the local judge.

Why be submissive? Paul gives several reasons.

First, the civil magistrate has God-given authority to punish violations of the law. He is a "minister [*diakanos* = servant] of God, a revenger to execute wrath upon him that doeth evil" (Rom. 13:4). "Vengeance is mine, I will repay, saith the Lord" (Rom. 12:19); God has absolute sovereign authority to revenge wrongs, but He has delegated a portion of that authority to the civil ruler. We obey the civil ruler, then, because we don't want to be punished as criminals.

The apparent tension between Romans 12 and Romans 13 must be noted. In Romans 12 Paul tells believers to "recompense to no man evil for evil" (v. 17) and to "avenge not yourselves" (v. 19). Yet Romans 13 says the civil ruler is a "revenger" (v. 4). The difference lies in the delegated authority given to civil rulers as compared to private citizens. Romans 12 addresses the relations of private citizens with each other; chapter 13 discusses the authority of civil rulers. "Vengeance is mine, I will repay, saith the Lord" (Rom. 12:19). God has absolute sovereign authority to revenge wrongs, but He has delegated a portion of that authority to civil rulers. Private citizens should be forgiving in their relations with one another and should not attempt to avenge wrongs. The civil ruler has a duty to avenge wrongs, because he has a responsibility to protect the innocent citizens under his charge. We have a saying in law, *"Minatur innocentibus qui parcit nocentibus"* [He threatens the innocent who spares the guilty]. This does not mean the civil ruler should never show mercy, but he must do so with due regard to the innocent victims of crime and the danger that judicial leniency will encourage further crime. The civil ruler needs to use his God-given authority, the sword he bears not in vain according to verse 4, to preserve law and order and to protect his citizens from aggression at home and abroad. In my view a major failure of the Carter administration was that President Carter, a professed born-again Christian, failed to distinguish between law and gospel and tried to govern according to Romans 12 when he should have governed according to Romans 13.

Second, we obey civil authority because those who disobey "shall receive to themselves damnation" (Rom. 13:2). This appears to refer to divine judgment. Even if you could commit the "perfect crime" and the police and prosecutors never catch you, God knows all things and you will not escape His divine discipline.

Third, we obey "not only for wrath, but also for conscience sake" (Rom. 13:5). Paul speaks of the works of the law written on men's hearts (Rom. 2:14-15), an inner sense of right and wrong that God has implanted in us. We often call this our conscience. Because of the Fall, conscience is far from infallible, but it is still a valuable tool in discerning right from wrong.

Conscience has been compared to a compass. A properly calibrated compass will reliably point to magnetic north. But with time a compass strays from accuracy and needs to be calibrated to point to magnetic north. There are machines for calibrating compasses.

The human conscience is like a compass, and the Bible is like a calibrator. Just as the compass is supposed to point to north, so the conscience is supposed to point to right and away from wrong. But as we stray from the Word of God, our conscience becomes warped and perverted. In fact, entire societies can become corrupt and depraved when the Word of God is forgotten. Just as we use a calibrator to correct an unreliable compass, so we correct a straying conscience by measuring it alongside the Word of God.

Conscience tells us we are to obey the civil authority because, first, he has divine authority, and, second, his laws are usually in accord with what is right. (What do we do when civil authority commands us to do what is wrong? See the next chapter.)

In addition to Paul's reasons for obeying civil authority—escaping criminal punishment, avoiding divine discipline, and heeding the voice of conscience—Peter gives us still another reason for obedience: "that with well doing ye may put to silence the ignorance of foolish men" (1 Pet. 2:15). At this time the enemies of Christianity were spreading false rumors about Christians—that Christians practiced cannibalism (a distortion of the Lord's Supper), that they refused to obey the laws, that they refused to fulfill the obligations of citizenship, that they were plotting the overthrow of the government, etc. The best way to disprove these rumors, Peter says, is to conduct yourselves like model citizens, going the second mile in fulfilling your civic duties.

As we will see in the next chapter, however, neither Paul nor Peter made obedience to civil authority an absolute. The time comes when we must obey God rather than man.

Still, a Christian response to President Clinton must include obedience to his lawful orders and to the statutes he and Congress enact and uphold, insofar as these are consistent with the higher laws of God.

Patriotism

Our response to President Clinton and to the nation he leads must go beyond grudging obedience. It must include patriotism as well.

Many of us found it easy to be patriotic during the Reagan era. President Reagan seemed to embody the very ideas and spirit that America was founded upon and that made America great. Those of us who were proud of America under President Reagan may find it harder to be patriotic while Clinton is president. For the spirit of the Clinton administration seems to embody the very antithesis of the Reagan era.

And yet, our patriotism must not slacken. In fact, our patriotism is needed today more than ever.

It could be easy for Christians to turn sour toward America during the next four years. As the programs of the Clinton administration unfold, Christians could easily assume that everything that was once right about America has been turned upside-down.

But Reagan was not 100 percent good, and Clinton is not 100 percent bad. (I would like to mention some good qualities and programs of the Clinton administration at this point. Just now I can't think of any, but I'm sure there must be some.)

And while we might like to think otherwise, Reagan did not speak for all of America. While he was president we still had the drug subculture, the gay subculture, the porn subculture, the liberal media, the permissive welfarist element—Reagan certainly did not speak for them!

Nor does President Clinton speak for all of America. Millions of Americans still hold traditional values. Bill Clinton does not speak for them! The fact that Clinton was elected does not necessarily mean the entire nation has abandoned traditional values, any more than the election of Reagan meant the entire nation had returned to those values.

In fact, while Reagan was elected in 1980 with 53 percent of the popular vote and reelected in 1984 with 59 percent, Clinton was elected in 1992 with only 43 percent. The fact is, 57 percent of the American electorate voted *against* Bill Clinton, even though he carefully disguised the more radical aspects of his liberal agenda and tried to pass himself off as a moderate!

The spirit of America is far from dead. The values that made this nation great may be in relapse, but they are not forgotten. The furor over gays in the military in January 1993, during which the White House hotlines received 450,000 calls per day overwhelmingly in opposition, many coming from veterans and others who had never been politically active before, proves that many Americans still hold traditional values.

When Clinton won the election 3 November, my greatest fear was that with the executive and legislative branches both in liberal hands, the entire Clinton agenda would sail through the Democrat-controlled Congress and become law. This has not happened, at least not to the extent I expected. Many congressmen and senators of the president's own party have shown a surprising independence—and several, like Sen. Richard Shelby (D-AL), have paid a price for doing so.

The point is, we must not give up on America! Much that is good and right about America still remains. We are still the bastion of freedom on earth, the leading nation of the free world. Our free enterprise economy, though crippled by deficit spending and government control, still managed to maintain a military force that held the Communist bloc at bay for half a century. (The Soviets produced a military machine roughly equal to our own; but their Socialist economy couldn't sustain it, and eventually it brought the whole system down.) And as communism collapses in the former Soviet Union and elsewhere, many nations look to the American system as a model for reconstruction.

Despite occasional clashes between church and state, Christians have more freedom in America than in almost any other nation. The Christian church in America is one of the world's strongest, and America sends out more missionaries and Bibles than any other nation in history.

Despite oppressive government control, Americans retain considerable freedom to choose their own vocations or businesses and run them as they see fit. We also retain the freedom to express our views and criticize our leaders, and while the neo-Fascist idea of "political correctness" has reared its ugly head on many campuses, its impact on the rest of society has thus far been quite limited. We retain the freedom to participate in the political process and influence the course of events. Millions of people in other nations would give everything they own to enjoy these freedoms.

Our system of justice is far from perfect. It is possible to get "railroaded" in an American court. But if I am accused of a crime, I'd still rather be tried in an American court of justice than in, say, Turkey or Mexico, wouldn't you?

Despite its imperfections, and despite the very real threats to our freedoms, America remains a great place to live. And on balance, America remains a force for good in the world.

In short, I'd still rather live in America—even Clinton's America—yes, probably even *Hillary* Clinton's America—than any other nation on earth.

Love of one's country is biblical. The Old Testament prophets burned with love for Israel, even while criticizing the nation's sins. Nehemiah, while holding an important position in the Persian government, still loved Israel so much that he left that position to rebuild the walls of Jerusalem. Esther, while serving as Persian queen, risked her life to save her people. Joseph served as prime minister of Egypt under Pharoah, but he refused to be buried there. The Israelites kept his bones in a coffin for four hundred years so they could carry them back to be buried in the Promised Land he loved. Jesus Himself loved His people and His city so much that He wept over them, "Jerusalem, Jerusalem, thou that killest the prophets" (Matt. 23:37).

Patriotism does not imply an absence of criticism. If we truly love our country we will criticize that which is wrong. But our criticism will be constructive, intended to correct and rebuild rather than destroy.

America needs our patriotism today more than ever. When the Supreme Court rules (5-4) that flagburning is a protected First Amendment right, let us wave our flag more proudly than ever. When a president who has himself dodged military service fails to return salutes to military personnel, or returns them sloppily, and a White House aide rebuffs a general's "good morning" with an abrupt "I don't talk to the military," let us make clear that these churlish words and actions do not speak for America as a whole.

Prayer

As Paul Cain rightly points out, the Apostle Paul exhorts us to pray for those in authority:

I exhort, therefore, that, first of all, supplications, prayers, intercessions, and giving of thanks, be made for all men;

For kings, and for all that are in authority; that we may lead a quiet and peaceable life in all godliness and honesty. (1 Tim. 2:1-2)

Paul wrote these words to Timothy sometime around A.D. 64, again while Nero was on the throne. Timothy was probably in Ephesus at the time, which is in Asia Minor and was part of the Roman Empire. Clearly, then, the exhortation is to pray for the Emperor Nero, as well as others in authority all the way down to the local magistrates. The reason—"that we may lead a quiet and peaceable life in all godliness and honesty"—clearly reflects the legitimate governmental function of keeping the peace and preserving law and order.

Paul mentions four types of petitions: supplications, prayers, intercessions, and giving of thanks. Each of these is to be employed on behalf of civil rulers. Supplications [*deesis* in the Greek] are requests made out of a recognition of dire need. Prayers [*proseuche*] are all-encompassing and refer to all forms of prayer or other requests to God. Intercessions [*enteuxis*] are requests made to a superior (God) on behalf of someone else, in this instance civil rulers. Giving of thanks [*eucharistia*] is an expression of gratitude, in this instance recognizing that God has ordained civil rulers over us for our benefit.

The all-encompassing nature of Paul's exhortation includes prayers not only for leaders we like and approve, but for those of the opposite character as well. One might argue that leaders who do not hold Christian values need our prayers more than those who do!

It goes without saying, then, that prayer for a president does not imply political support. If you are a rock-ribbed Republican, you are not being disloyal by praying for a Democrat. I seriously doubt that Paul would have voted for Nero, but he exhorted prayer for Nero nevertheless!

Nor is there any inconsistency in praying, "Lord, please give President Clinton your wisdom and guidance to make the decisions he must make as our leader. And please motivate us to work harder next election to vote him out of office and replace him with someone better!"

Remember, though, God does answer prayer. "The king's heart is in the hand of the Lord, as the rivers of water: he turneth it whithersoever he will" (Prov. 21:1). God can and does change the hearts of rulers. As an attorney I have fought in packed courtrooms and legislative chambers for the causes of churches and Christian families, and I believe the judges and legislators were influenced by the prayers of believers.

One danger of praying for a leader you don't like is that God might answer your prayer and change him so much that you'll have a hard time voting against him in the next election. But that's a risk I'm willing to take!

Support as Spokesman for America

Whatever you and I may think of President Clinton, he does represent our nation in the eyes of the world. In a sense, when he speaks for America he speaks for all of us.

And as the chief executive of the nation he administers the normal and legitimate functions of government. Even under a demented emperor like Nero, the normal and legitimate functions of government—law enforcement, national defense, economic policy, resource conservation, etc.—continued, at least after a fashion. In fulfilling these functions, the president is entitled to our cooperation and support.

Communication

Whether we approve or disapprove of President Clinton and his policies, the channels of communication must be kept open.

As president, Bill Clinton must communicate with diverse segments of the American people. That includes elements of society with which he does not necessarily agree. That may even include conservative Christians.

Christians need not, must not hide their opposition to various aspects of the Clinton agenda. But we must keep the lines of communication open, so our ideas will at least be considered.

As we try to be "salt of the earth" and "light unto the world," we can be salt and light even to the Clinton administration. This is one reason why, in confronting the Clinton agenda, it is better to address issues and policies rather than personalities.

chapter 5

Loyal *Opposition*: The Role of Opposition

In England for the past century or so, the political scene has been dominated by the Conservative party and the Labour party. When one party is in power, the other party is traditionally referred to as the "loyal opposition."

This term summarizes the role of the party out of power. They are loyal to the nation and to the elected leadership which represents the nation. For example, during both world wars both parties pulled together to help England win the war. But they also fill a role of opposition because they actively oppose those policies which they sincerely believe are wrong and not in the national interest. In so doing they help keep the administration on its toes, because they stand ready to exploit instances of incompetence or corruption.

The previous chapter focused on *loyalty*. This chapter focuses on *opposition*.

As we saw in chapter 4, Romans 13 teaches that the civil ruler is the "minister of God to thee for good" (v. 4). Insofar as he fulfills that role, we have a duty to obey and be loyal.

But what if the leader corrupts his role? What if he ceases to be a minister for good and becomes a minister for evil instead? What if, instead of rewarding good and punishing evil, he rewards evil and punishes good? Do we still support him? Do we show loyalty to him? Do we even obey him?

Sir William Blackstone, whose *Commentaries on the Laws of England* was widely read in colonial America and shaped the founding fathers' understanding of law, spoke of the "Revealed Law" which comes from God and which is "found only in the Holy Scriptures," and the "Law of Nature" which is "dictated by God Himself." "Upon these two foundations," he said, "the law of nature and the law of revelation, depend all human laws; that is to say, no human law should be suffered to contradict these." Human law, he said, is "a rule of civil conduct prescribed by the supreme power in a state . . . commanding what is right, and prohibiting what is wrong." But what if government enacts laws which are contrary to the law of revelation and the law of nature, and which command what is wrong and prohibit what is right? Should they be obeyed?

In a representative society such as ours, where we elect our leaders and exercise some influence over government policy, opposition can take place on several levels.

Selective and Constructive Criticism

One level is selective and constructive criticism. We might adopt this posture when we basically support a leader but are not 100 percent pleased with his performance.

Many evangelicals felt this way about George Bush. They voted for him in large numbers in 1988 and wanted him to win reelection in 1992. They were generally proud of his handling of Desert Storm and were thankful for his uncompromising pro-life stance, but were frustrated by his failure to articulate a clear conservative vision for America the way his predecessor Ronald Reagan had.

While generally supportive, they criticized certain of his appointments and policies. They did so, not to bring the Bush administration down to defeat, but rather to correct certain aspects of his policy. Most conservative Christians were genuinely disappointed when President Bush did not win reelection.

Total Political Opposition

A second level is total political opposition. When we take this approach, we have decided to go beyond selectively and constructively opposing certain aspects and policies of the administration. We have decided that the administration is beyond reforming, that the nation would be better off without this administration, and so we work actively for the administration's defeat.

There is obviously a difference between selective and constructive criticism, and total political opposition. When Christians engaged in constructive criticism of certain Bush policies, we were (or should have been) careful to ensure that our criticism would not hurt Bush's chances for reelection. We recognized that while George Bush's views and policies were not completely in accord with our own, they were far better than those of his likely opponents. But when we engage in total political opposition to the Clinton administration, we have concluded that the best interest of the nation requires his defeat.

Normally, this level of opposition is exercised by working for the administration's defeat in the next election. In extreme circumstances, we might seek the president's impeachment. Grounds for impeachment, according to Article 2 section 4 of the Constitution, include "Treason, Bribery, or other high Crimes and Misdemeanors" (stupidity is not listed). First a majority of the House of Representatives must vote Articles of Impeachment, and then two-thirds of the Senate must vote for conviction. While impeachment is a drastic remedy, it is a check upon executive power which the Founding Fathers placed in the Constitution.

Even while we disagree with this leader's policies, we believe he is ordained by the permissive will of God according to Romans 13. We therefore obey his laws and orders while he is in office.

In short, we use all political means of opposition, but we operate within the law. We work in and through the political process, using persuasion, media, organization, etc., to bring about this leader's defeat and the election of someone better. But we do not go beyond the law.

Selective Civil Disobedience

A third level is selective civil disobedience. Those who adopt this approach have concluded that, at least in some respects, laws exist that require them to do what God forbids, or forbid them to do what God requires, and that they must obey God rather than men.

When Christians adopt this approach, they have not necessarily concluded that the administration is evil in every respect. But they have determined that at least one aspect of administration policy is contrary to the law of God and that they cannot in good conscience obey it.

We have already seen that Romans 13 and 1 Peter 2 impose a strong obligation to obey civil authorities, even when the civil government is a corrupt pagan welfare state like Rome, and even when the ruler is a demented persecutor like Nero.

But the duty of obedience is not absolute. Paul himself probably wrote the Book of Romans from the Corinthian jail, having disobeyed the civil authorities by preaching the gospel; and Peter was frequently jailed for preaching in defiance of civil law. His answer when told to stop preaching was, "We ought to obey God rather than men" (Acts 5:29).

Therein lies the fundamental principle which underlies biblical civil disobedience: We obey civil authority except when the authorities command us to do what the Word of God forbids, or forbid us to do what the Word of God commands.

The effort to rescue babies from abortion is a case in point. If, as I believe the Scripture clearly teaches, the unborn child is a living human being, then abortion constitutes premeditated killing of innocent human life. Pro-life advocates have worked actively for the adoption of laws that protect the unborn child. At level one of our analysis they have engaged in constructive criticism of laws that allow abortion and have sought to change those laws. But while they have had some successes in restricting abortion and particularly (until the Clinton administration) in cutting off most abortion funding, abortion remains legal.

So pro-life advocates have gone to level two, total political opposition, actively working for the election of pro-life candidates and the defeat of officeholders who are pro-abortion. Again they have achieved some successes, but even pro-life officeholders are limited in what they can do. The Supreme Court, in the recent 5-

4 *Planned Parenthood v. Casey* decision (1992), ruled that while the states can regulate abortion to a far greater extent than was previously believed, they cannot completely prohibit abortion. The killing therefore goes on.

Some pro-life advocates have therefore gone a step further. Besides using the political process to elect pro-life candidates and enact pro-life legislation, and using the right of free expression to persuade people that abortion is wrong, these people have literally placed their bodies on the line for the pro-life cause. Physically blocking access to abortuaries to save babies from being aborted, they have technically violated the criminal trespass laws and have therefore gone to level three, selective civil disobedience. They call these activities "rescue," not protest, because they have gone beyond persuasion and seek to save babies' lives by force if necessary. By way of analogy, they say, if you saw someone who was about to commit murder, you wouldn't just try to talk him out of it; you'd stop him by force if possible. Abortion, they argue convincingly, is just as much murder as the killing of any other human being. They point to the midwives' refusal to obey Pharoah's command to kill Hebrew children (Exod. 1) and Esther's acts of disobedience to save her people (Esther 4).

I call these actions *civil* disobedience because rescuers do not engage in violent resistance. With few exceptions they submit to arrest and either go willingly with the police to jail, or else they go limp and allow themselves to be dragged or carried to jail. But they do not fight back against the police.

I call these activities *selective* civil disobedience because these rescuers are not engaged in general disobedience or crime. Most rescuers are patriotic, hard-working citizens who have clean criminal records except for rescue activity. They have chosen to disobey the law which allows abortion, and this law alone, because they believe this law is in conflict with the Word of God which commands them to rescue innocent unborn children.

But these are acts of disobedience nevertheless.

Others practice civil disobedience in other contexts. Some refuse to pay income tax, either because they believe the tax itself is immoral and/or unconstitutional, or because their consciences will not allow them to pay tax monies which are used by the government to finance abortion or anti-Christian forms of education. (In previous decades persons on the other side of the ideological spectrum refused to pay taxes to subsidize the Vietnam War.) Some Christian-school and home-school parents have defied state officials, and a few have gone to jail, rather than submit their children to the influence of public education or accept coercive and intrusive state regulation of home and private schools. Most noteworthy of these were the "Louisville Seven," Christian fathers who endured jail sentences and withstood Nebraska authorities in the early 1980s. Christians still debate whether the Louisville Seven were right or wrong in their civil disobedience, but few will deny that, partially as a result of their courageous stand, the climate for home schooling and private schools is much more favorable than it was a decade ago. As an attorney who has represented numerous private schools and home-school families and who has testified before many legislatures and governors' commissions concerning home- and private-school legislation, I have found public officials much more willing to listen since the Louisville Seven took their stand. "We don't want another Louisville, Nebraska, situation here in our state" is their common refrain.

It is difficult to know where to draw the line on civil disobedience. If blocking entry to abortion clinics to save the lives of innocent children is justifiable, how about sabotaging the clinic by bombing it or torching it? After all, aren't babies' lives worth more than property?

These are difficult questions. One factor to consider is that violence begets violence. Violent action against abortion clinics can be expected to result in violation reprisals against right-to-life offices and crisis pregnancy centers.

One blessing of America is that we can usually resolve our differences by legal and political means. We normally limit ourselves to operating within these means, and we can usually expect our opponents to do likewise. This practice has contributed greatly to the stability of our nation and has usually made it possible for us to resolve our differences without having to resort to force or violence. If this expectation is broken down, America will have lost one of its greatest strengths. For this reason, disobeying the law—in fact, even civil disobedience—should be regarded as a last resort.

Removal by Force

A fourth level of resistance is rarely if ever justified: removal by force. This might take the form of a small coup d'état by a few people, or a popular revolution, or, commonly, something in between. Frequently, through clever propaganda and careful manipulation of the media, a small coup d'état is made to look like a popular revolution.

Our perspective on revolution varies with the situation. Rebels who meet with our approval are called "patriots" and "freedom fighters"; those of whom we disapprove are called "traitors" and "subversives." Looking back upon history, it might even be said that patriots are traitors who succeeded, and traitors are patriots who failed.

Generally, though, rebellion against authority is condemned by Scripture. The terms "rebel," "rebelled," "rebellest," "rebellion," "rebellious," and "rebels" are found approximately one hundred times in the Bible, and almost without exception the terms are used disapprovingly. Usually they connote rebellion against God; sometimes they connote rebellion against his civil servants. Since Christians are generally commanded to support civil authority, rebellion is normally against the will of God.

And rebellion usually doesn't work. Usually it fails, and simply brings bloodshed and disorder. If it succeeds in overthrowing the government, it usually replaces that government with another that turns out to be worse. Witness the French Revolution that led to anarchy and chaos and a bloodbath that lasted until Napoleon finally restored order, or the Soviet revolution that brought horror to Russia for most of this century. Rebels usually come to power promising freedom, justice, equality, democracy, and prosperity; but shortly after seizing power they are likely to become just as totalitarian, just as unfair, and just as inept as they accuse their predecessors of being. Every Communist government in history has been proof of that. There is an old saying, "Under capitalism man exploits his fellow man; under communism it's the reverse." Consider the rebellion of Jeroboam and the ten northern tribes of Israel against Solomon's son Rehoboam (1 Kings 11-13). Even though many of their grievances against Rehoboam were legitimate, Jeroboam and his successors turned out to be just as bad or worse.

There may be circumstances in which revolution is the only alternative. A government may become so totally corrupt, so totally destructive of the legitimate ends of government, that revolution may be either a positive good or a necessary evil. For Christians living in Nazi Germany or Stalinist Russia, a well-timed and well-planned coup with a realistic chance of succeeding might have been an appropriate Christian response.

But before deciding upon that course of action, would-be revolutionaries should carefully consider the consequences. Is the government really so destructive of the legitimate ends of government that revolution and all its attendant evils are justified? Does the revolution have a realistic chance of succeeding? And if it does succeed, do we have something better to put in place of the existing government?

During the 1960s anti-war activist Tom Hayden (formerly Mr. Jane Fonda) spoke at a "student power" rally at the University of Iowa. One student asked what type of government he and his comrades planned after the revolution. He answered in effect, "Let's not worry about that for now. Right now let's concentrate on the revolution, and we'll worry about that afterwards."

He had good reason to be evasive. His audience consisted of revolutionaries with widely different agendas. Some were Communists, others Socialists, others Anarchists, others trade union Syndicalists, among many others. They knew and were united on what they were revolting against, but not what they were revolting for. If Hayden had revealed his plans, he would have lost much of his support. Cunning, but totally irresponsible! If his revolution had succeeded, there would have been nothing but civil war between the competing factions.

What of the American Revolution, you ask? Suffice it to say that in my view this was not a revolution but rather a War for Independence. (For a full discussion of the legal and moral case for this position, see my book, *God and Caesar* [Wheaton, Ill.: Crossway, 1984, 1992], 33-35.)

Which of these four levels of opposition is the appropriate Christian response to the Clinton agenda? Selective constructive criticism? Total political opposition? Selective civil disobedience? Removal by force?

Clearly the last of these is uncalled for. For all its faults, the Clinton administration is still carrying out the basic functions of government—law enforcement, national defense (after a fashion), etc.

And unlike some countries in which leaders hold office for life, Americans can register their dissatisfaction at the polls in 1994, electing a Congress that will be more resistant to the Clinton agenda. And in 1996, if the Clinton administration hasn't shaped up, we can vote them out of office.

As to the remaining three possibilities, we must remember that the civil ruler is ordained of God, to reward those who do good and punish those who do evil. Has the Clinton administration betrayed this mandate to the point of rewarding evil and punishing good?

Consider the following:

(1) The administration is trying to admit those who engage in sodomous conduct—not just an alternate lifestyle, but one positively declared sinful by the Word of God—into military service, thus giving them one of the highest forms of legitimacy our society can give. Open or suspected homosexuals serve in cabinet and subcabinet level positions in the Clinton administration. The Family Research Council reports that openly gay Bob Hattoy, the Deputy Director of Presidential Personnel, is giving special treatment to homosexual applicants for government posts.

(2) Our national security is being weakened as our military forces are scaled down beyond what experts recommend as wise; fine career personnel are being forced out as the administration seeks to make room for homosexuals. Equally important, if not more so, the right of the American people to be militarily secure from foreign aggression is being jeopardized.

(3) President Clinton has tried, unsuccessfully so far, to eliminate the ban on admitting HIV-positive immigrants into the United States, thus adding a health danger to Americans and an added taxpayers' expense.

(4) The administration is pressing for passage of the Freedom of Choice Act by which the "right" to abortion on demand at any stage of pregnancy will be protected by federal law. The bill is a misnomer. Babies have no choice in this life-and-death decision. Fathers cannot choose to protect the lives of their soon-to-be-aborted children. States have no choice as to what their respective laws in this area shall be. This bill simply forces the pro-abortion position down everyone's throat.

(5) Not only will unborn babies not be protected;

their killers will be paid by federal funds. The Clinton administration wants to renew federal funding of abortions. (With priorities like these, no wonder there is a crisis in paying for health care!)

(6) President Clinton is also taking steps to allow abortions in military hospitals and to provide abortion coverage on government workers' insurance plans.

(7) The administration also seeks legislation allowing experimentation on live and dead fetuses—some of it at taxpayers' expense!

(8) By order of President Clinton, federally funded counselors may now advise women to have their babies killed. The regulations prohibiting such counseling, though upheld as constitutional in *Rust v. Sullivan* (1991), were removed by a stroke of the Clinton pen last January.

(9) The Clinton administration is pushing legislation to impose added criminal penalties for those who block abortion clinics. This is a clear form of content-based discrimination, as no such penalties are proposed for those who block right-to-life centers or other facilities.

(10) Though candidate Clinton promised an $800 per-child tax credit, President Clinton has forgotten that pledge and now wants to eliminate the Young Child Tax Credit—a measure that imposes an added tax burden upon the traditional family.

(11) As another blow to the traditional family, President Clinton's proposed tax increase resurrects the "marriage penalty" which had been corrected by the Reagan administration in the 1986 Tax Reform Act. Under the Clinton proposal, two people living together and making a combined income of $140,000 would each pay $5,425 less in federal taxes as single people living together than they would have to pay if they got married. Clinton's tax policy rewards people for living in sin and punishes them for doing the right thing and getting married.

(12) The proposed tax increases, besides being a

broken campaign promise, are a severe and unjustified burden upon American citizens, typical of those imposed by Rehaboam upon his people (1 Kings 12).

In these and many other areas, it seems clear that the Clinton administration is moving the nation in an unwholesome direction. The weight of the federal government is being placed on the side of gay rights, abortion, and many other evils. In many respects, President Clinton seeks to punish that which is good and reward that which is evil.

Constructive criticism is necessary, but it is not enough. The Clinton administration seems determined to move the nation in a direction that is diametrically at odds with the Word of God and the traditional Judeo-Christian values upon which the nation was founded. Christians and others who hold traditional values should begin now to work for the defeat of President Clinton and the election of a better president in 1996 and, before that, the election in 1994 of a Congress that will resist the Clinton agenda. The alternative will be national disaster—politically, economically, militarily, morally, and spiritually unless the Clinton Administration dramatically changes course in the near future.

In certain respects, such as abortion, selective civil disobedience may be appropriate as well. But in a free and representative society such as ours, the main emphasis should be upon legal and political action.

So what should we do? We need a broad, aggressive, positive plan of action for the Clinton years.

Interested? See the next chapter: "A Victory Plan for Conservative Christians During the Clinton Era."

chapter 6

A Victory Plan for Conservative Christians during the Clinton Era

It was election night, 1984. After a hard-fought campaign, Ronald Reagan had just been reelected with 59 percent of the vote and forty-nine of fifty states.

Having worked hard in Reagan's campaign, I rejoiced in his victory, but I was especially intrigued by his opponent's concession speech. Urging his supporters not to be discouraged, Walter Mondale assured them, "In every defeat are the seeds of victory, and in every victory are the seeds of defeat."

Mondale's words are a reminder that, just as America was not removed from its traditional values overnight, so it cannot be returned to those values in a single day, or year, or term of office. Rather, the battle to preserve our basic values (or restore them, depending upon how far gone you think this nation is) is a continuing struggle with neither beginning nor end.

Some Christians naively plunge into a political campaign viewing it as one cataclysmic Armageddon-like battle between good and evil, and once the beast is defeated and bound we will all be able to sit back and enjoy the millennium for the next thousand years. Too often, we assume the problems which beset America began with Michael Dukakis, or Walter Mondale, or back during the New Deal era of Franklin D. Roosevelt, or perhaps during the years of Wilsonian democracy, or maybe during the regime of Lincoln (or, depending on your region of the country, the Confederacy and slavery), or possibly back to Jefferson and the freethinkers (or, depending on your point of view, Hamilton and the bankers). In fact, the seeds of apostasy were present from the very founding of this Christian republic, and they will be with us throughout human history. The objective of the battle for traditional values is not to eliminate apostasy but to keep it in check. And this side of heaven and/or Christ's millennial rule, the battle will never be over. I welcome Christians into the political arena for whatever term they're willing to stay, but my highest admiration is for those brave, seasoned soldiers who stand firm for the long haul.

I remember the first presidential campaign in which I was intensively involved. The year was 1964, and I respected Barry Goldwater and his stand on the issues. The notes he sounded during his campaign rung responsive chords in my heart: an end to big government, permissiveness, welfarism, socialism, appeasement of communism. I served as vice-chairman of Students for Goldwater at St. Olaf College, and during the campaign I spent far more time working at headquarters than studying for my classes. When on election day Goldwater suffered a crushing defeat, no one was more heartbroken than I. The media confidently proclaimed that the conservative movement was dead, and with it perhaps the Republican party as well.

But the obituaries were premature, for Goldwater was a man ahead of his time. The themes of Goldwater's campaign stirred the hearts of many who carried them forward—including a civic-minded actor named Ronald Reagan who made speeches on Goldwater's behalf. Two years later, echoing Goldwater's campaign themes, Republicans made significant gains, and Reagan was elected governor of California. Two years after that, in 1968, a moderate conservative named Richard Nixon was elected president. When Nixon was reelected with 61 percent of the vote and forty-nine states, pundits said the Democratic party was dead.

But, echoing Mondale's words, the Nixon landslide of 1972 carried with it the seeds of defeat—Watergate. Two years later Nixon was out of office, the Democrats made substantial gains in '74 and '76, and the media again said the Republicans were dead.

But 1980 saw the election of Ronald Reagan. When Reagan won reelection in 1984 with forty-nine of fifty states, the Reagan Revolution was in full swing and the media again spoke of the death of liberalism. The "Revolution" continued with the election of Bush in 1988.

During those twelve years we didn't solve all of the nation's ills—far from it. But we did make substantial progress. Inflation and interest rates were cut drastically. Our national defense became relatively stronger, and the Communist advance that had swallowed nation after nation in the 1970s came to a screeching halt; after 1981 the Communists failed to gain a single inch of territory anywhere in the world, and by 1990 the "evil empire" had begun to crumble. The liberal majority on the Supreme Court that had led the way in moving the nation to the Left during the sixties by legalizing abortion and outlawing school prayer and other forms of public religious expression had been balanced by conservative appointments. While it cannot be said that the Court has a true conservative majority, the Court's make-up is far different from what it was in the 1960s, and in 1992 we came only one vote short (5-4) of overturning the 8-1 prayer decision and the 7-2 abortion decision of an earlier era. The days of *Roe v. Wade*, it seemed, were numbered.

But in 1992, with Perot in the race as a third candidate, Bill Clinton was elected president and the Reagan Revolution came to a screeching halt.

Or did it?

The problems that beset America—big government, the welfare state, appeasement of communism, decay of traditional values—go back to the New Deal days of the 1930s, and in fact before that. And the Reagan Revolution against big government et al. did not begin in 1980. It began with Goldwater in 1964, gained impetus with the election of Nixon in 1968, was temporarily derailed by Watergate in the seventies, went into full steam under Reagan and Bush in the eighties, and has now suffered a temporary setback with the election of Clinton. But it is far from over! The fact that Clinton is a minority president elected with only 43 percent of the vote, that his standing in the polls at this point in his term is the lowest of any president in modern history, that a national furor arose when he tried to force homosexuals upon the military, are proof that traditional values are very much alive in America today.

No question about it, we suffered a defeat in 1992. For the next four years those who hold traditional values will not hold power in the executive and legislative branches of the federal government. But how do we respond to that defeat? We can feel sorry for ourselves and become disillusioned with the whole political process. Or we can recognize the truth of Mondale's words, and look for the seeds of victory in the 1992 defeat. If we view the Clinton era as a temporary vacation from national power, as a time for conservative Christians to reflect, rethink, retrench, regroup, and rejuvenate, we can lay the groundwork for a resounding victory in 1996 and the years to come.

So how do we bring about this victory? Let me suggest some basic thoughts, first for the individual and then for the church, and then let me itemize some priorities and ideas concerning the important issues of our day.

The Individual

It is sometimes said that the whole is equal to the sum of its parts. In a sense, the moral and spiritual health and strength of the nation consists of the combined moral and spiritual health and strength of the many individual citizens who make up the nation.

However, it is also true that a disciplined, organized, and motivated minority can direct the course of a nation. At no time during the history of the Soviet Union had the Communist party ever numbered more than 5 percent of the population; yet they seized power, held power, ruled, and almost ruined the nation for over seventy years. Likewise an organized, motivated, and disciplined cadre of Christian believers can exert an influence in America far in excess of our numbers.

Remember the "salt of the earth" principle—it takes only a small amount of salt to flavor your steak. You don't put steak on your salt (though some have accused me of doing that!); you put salt on your steak. And you don't say your salt tastes "steaky"; you say your steak tastes salty. Salt permeates our food and gives it a flavoring far out of proportion to its volume. But a nation cannot have too much salt.

We can speak of national repentance and revival. In the final analysis a nation cannot repent and revive; only individuals can. But if enough individuals repent and revive, it affects the nation as a whole and looks like a national revival!

We must begin, then, by building individual believers who learn sound doctrine, practice it in their lives, and apply it to our society. We must preach conversion through the power of the Holy Spirit leading people to trust Jesus Christ and the salvation He procured for us by dying for our sins on the Cross. The "social gospel" is no gospel at all; social reform without the prior regenerating power of God on the heart of the individual is at best a temporary improvement. And a profession of salvation without a changed life is like seed sown among thorns. Too many of us have crusaded to reform society without making sure our own lives are squared away first.

In 1982, Congress and President Reagan declared 1983 the "Year of the Bible." While I applaud this gesture, we live in a society in which the Bible is revered by many, read by few, understood by fewer, and practiced by fewer still. We need to recapture the full-orbed faith of our Puritan forefathers who applied the Bible to every aspect of their lives—including civil government.

For the Bible does address the civic issues of our day. Practically every issue you can imagine—abortion, economics, social responsibility, debt, interest, property rights, education, crime, capital punishment, war, and military service to name but a few—is addressed at least in principle in the Bible. The Bible is as relevant to modern society as tomorrow's newspaper—in fact, more so!

Believers therefore need to get into the Word and study its application. While obviously this means the application of the Bible to every aspect of our lives, in this context I am speaking of its application to civil government and the issues of our day. The appendix, "Can Dispensationalists and Reconstructionists Work Together? Yes, If They Read Luther!" was written to help Christians understand how to apply biblical principles of government to the problems of modern society.

To help understand what the Bible says about government and political issues, I have written *God and Caesar: Christian Faith and Political Action* (Wheaton, Ill.: Crossway, 1984, 1992), which explains in biblical terms the purposes of government, our responsibilities toward government, and a biblical position on issues like economics, the family, abortion, education, censorship and pornography, crime and punishment, war, military service, and international relations. My book *Christianity and the Constitution: The Faith of Our Founding Fathers* (Grand Rapids, MI: Baker, 1987, 1993), documents the religious beliefs of the founders of our nation and shows how Christianity influenced our constitutional form of government. My ten-hour tape series, "The Institute on the Constitution" (available through me at Jones School of Law, 5345 Atlanta Highway, Montgomery, AL 36193), explains the Christian beliefs of the founding fathers and contains a phrase-by-phrase explanation of the Constitution, what it says, what the framers meant by it, and how the courts have interpreted or misinterpreted it today. These are but a few of many tools that can help the reader or listener understand what the Bible says about civil government and the issues of today.

A veritable gold mine of current conservative books— and at discount prices!—is the Conservative Book Club (15 Oakland Avenue, Harrison, NY 10528). I strongly recommend that you join.

Numerous periodicals are available to keep you informed and give you a conservative and/or Christian perspective on the news. Among the best traditional conservative periodicals are *National Review* (P.O. Box 96636, Washington, D.C. 20078-7471); *American Spectator* (2020 N. 14th St., Suite 750, Arlington, VA 22216); *Conservative Chronicle* (Box 11297-NR, Des Moines, IA 50340-1297); *New American* (770 Westhill Blvd., Appleton, WI 54915); and *Human Events* (422 1st St. S.E., Washington, D.C. 20003). An excellent daily newspaper with a nationwide mail circulation is the *Washington Times*

(3600 New York Ave. N.E., Washington, D.C. 20002).

Periodicals which present the news from a distinctively Christian standpoint include Focus on the Family's *Citizen* (Colorado Springs, CO 80995); *Christian Crusade* (P.O. Box 977, Tulsa, OK 74102); American Vision's *Biblical Worldview* (P.O. Box 724088, Atlanta, GA 30339-1088); *Christian News* (Box 168, New Haven, MO. 63068); *Forerunner* (P.O. Box 1799, Gainesville, FL 32602); and Christian Coalition's *Christian American* (1801-L Sara Drive, Chesapeake, VA 23320). *National Right to Life News*, published by National Right to Life (Suite 500, 419 7th St., N.W., Washington, D.C. 20004), is an excellent source of information on breaking developments on abortion and related issues.

Several newsletters provide hard-hitting factual information. Founded by former top White House aide Gary Bauer, the Family Research Council publishes *Washington Watch* (700 13th Street, N.W., Suite 500, Washington, D.C. 20005-3960, 800-232-6459). A different organization with a similar name, the Family Research Institute, headed by Dr. Paul Cameron, publishes the *Family Research Report* (P.O. Box 2091, Washington, D.C. 20013), which features detailed statistical research on issues pertaining to homosexuality. Dr. Fred Schwarz, founder of the Christian Anti-Communism Crusade (P.O. Box 890, Long Beach, CA 90801-0890), publishes an informative newsletter that focuses upon foreign policy but also deals with AIDS and other relevant topics. David Horowitz, a former New Left activist who has matured into a leading conservative intellectual, publishes a magazine called *Heterodoxy* (Center for Popular Culture, 12400 Ventura Blvd., Suite 304, Studio City, CA 91604, 800-752-6562), which pointedly refutes the arguments of the homosexual movement and features somewhat irreverent attacks upon the "politically correct" movement in academia.

Phyllis Schlafly, founder of Eagle Forum (Box 618, Alton, IL 62002), publishes the *Phyllis Schlafly Report* and the *Education Reporter*, both of which are excellent newsletters. Another good conservative newsletter is the *McAlvany Intelligence Advisor* (P.O. Box 84904, Phoenix, AZ 85071), in which Don McAlvany provides up-to-date information on a variety of subjects with special emphasis on economics and finance. Still another is *Imprimis*, a thought-provoking conservative newsletter produced by Hillsdale College (Hillsdale, MI 49242). Dr. D. James Kennedy's *Washington Newsletter* (Coral Ridge Ministries, 5555 North Federal Highway, Ft. Lauderdale, FL 33308) is always well researched and well thought out. And one more: *Legacy*, the scholarly and penetrating newsletter of Dr. George Grant (Legacy Communications, P.O. Box 680365, Franklin, TN 37068).

Several foundations produce highly scholarly and well-documented conservative research reports. Among these are the Cato Institute (224 2nd St. S.E., Washington, D.C. 20003) and the Heritage Foundation (214 Massachusetts Avenue, N.E., Washington, D.C. 20002; HF's *Policy Review* is a top-notch conservative publication).

Conservatives in academia should tune in to ISI, the Intercollegiate Studies Institute (14 South Bryn Mawr Ave., Bryn Mawr, PA 19010-3275, 800-526-7022). ISI's *Intercollegiate Review* is among the most scholarly journals published; their *University Bookman* contains excellent and timely book reviews; and their *Campus* magazine is a delightful gadfly exposing the hypocrisy of liberal-dominated "politically correct" academia.

This certainly is not a complete list of all good sources of information, but it is a good start. From these you can pick several that communicate well with you and give you the information you need. Remember, knowledge is power!

But becoming informed is not enough. Reading can make you the best-educated person in the concentration camp, but it won't make you a free person or this a free nation. Some Christians read extensively and become very well informed on the issues, but do nothing about their knowledge. This is like hiding your light under a bushel, or keeping your salt in the shaker! We should be "doers of the word, and not hearers only" (James 1:22).

As concerned Christian citizens we should not hesitate to express our views on the issues, tactfully but forthrightly. We need to call in to the talk shows and present our views and write letters to editors and to our elected officials. Several quick tips about letter writing:

(1) Be brief. Letters more than about a page in length will probably not be printed in newspapers or read by legislators.

(2) Be courteous. Don't threaten to ruin his career for life if he doesn't vote your way. He knows you feel strongly or you wouldn't have written. It does help, however, to multiply the influence of your letter by stressing whom you represent. Rather than speaking for yourself only, it sounds better to sign your letter "Mr. and Mrs." if you can. Or if you can say "As pastor of a church with 500 average weekly attendance" or "As president of an organization with 1,000 members," your legislator will know that you are in a position to influence other voters.

(3) Be accurate. If your facts are incorrect, you and your cause will lose credibility. It is also important to use good grammar, spelling and punctuation; if you are unsure in this area, have someone proofread your letter before you send it. And if you are writing to a legislator it helps to refer to the bill by number. If you can say Senate Bill #109, he can find it in a couple of minutes; if he doesn't know what bill you are referring to, your letter may be lost in the shuffle.

America has generally operated on a two-party system. While third parties have occasionally had some influence, normally you have to work with one of the two major parties. I encourage Christians to attend the precinct caucus of the party of their choice; you can find out when and where it is held by calling party headquarters or the local voter registration office at the courthouse. The precinct caucus is where grassroots politics begins, where the resolutions and endorsements are formulated that eventually make up the county, state, and national party platforms. Attending your precinct caucus gives you the opportunity to become a delegate to your county and state conventions, or serve as a precinct officer.

Even if you don't care to work for a particular political party, you can volunteer to help in a particular candidate's campaign. You might select a candidate based upon his character and integrity, his qualifications for the office he seeks, and particularly his stand on the issues as proven by his past voting record. By calling the candidate or his campaign headquarters and volunteering to help, you will be given plenty to do.

You can stand on a soapbox on Main Street and orate about the issues of the day, and you might convert a person here and there. But to be really effective in American politics it is usually necessary to organize, to work in concert with like-minded people.

Many good conservative and Christian organizations exist. Focus on the Family, the radio ministry founded by Dr. James Dobson, has established organizations in most of the fifty states to work for pro-family causes; these organizations have different names in different states. You can write to Focus at Colorado Springs, CO 80995, to find out how to contact their organization in your state.

Christian Coalition, established by Pat Robertson, likewise has chapters in various states and localities. Their national headquarters is 1801-L Sara Drive, Chesapeake, VA 23320. They, too, are a conservative organization dedicated to preserving the Christian values that made America great.

The Plymouth Rock Foundation (14 McKinley Circle, Marlborough, NH 03455) is establishing Committees of Correspondence (Comcors) in various states to promote understanding of the Christian principles that underlie our constitutional heritage.

Eagle Forum, one of the nation's most effective conservative groups, is organized in all fifty states; their national offices may be contacted at 68 Fairmount, Alton, IL 62002. Another is Concerned Women for America, 370 L'Enfant Promenade, Suite 800, Washington, D.C. 20024. Eagle Forum and CWA are often perceived as women's groups, but they have many male members as well.

Two more conservative organizations deserve special mention—the Free Congress Foundation (717 2nd St. N.E., Washington, D.C. 20002), because of its outstanding record of contributions to the conservative cause, and Empower America (1776 I Street, N.W., Suite 890, Washington, D.C. 20006), because of its promise for the future.

These organizations work for conservative causes generally. Others are organized to work for single issues, and they too are an important part of the political scene. National Right to Life is one of the most effective pro-life organizations, with chapters in all fifty states. To find out how to reach your state chapter, contact the national office at 419 7th St., N.W., Washington, D.C. 20004.

Several organizations are working actively to preserve a strong national defense, particularly in light of the Clinton cuts and the proposed lifting of the gay ban. These include the Center for Military Readiness (P.O. Box 2324, Livonia, MI 48151); Officers' Christian Fellowship (P.O. Box 1177, Englewood, CO 80150); and High Frontier (20800 Shirlington, Suite 405A, Arlington, VA 22206).

The National Association for the Self-Employed (2121 Precinct Line Road, Suite 100, Hurst, TX 76054, 800-232-NASE) lobbies actively for small business, for the free enterprise system, and against excessive government regulation. NASE membership makes one eligible for many substantial benefits, including health insurance and scholarship aid.

Several legal organizations serve as counterweights to groups like the ACLU, defending churches and individual Christians against infringements upon their religious liberty. These include the Rutherford Institute (1445 East Rio Road, Charlottesville, VA 22901); the National Legal Foundation (6477 College Park Square, Suite 306, Virginia Beach, VA 23464, 800-397-4242); the Christian Legal Society (4208 Evergreen Avenue, Suite 222, Annandale, VA 22003); and the American Family Association (P.O. Drawer 2440, Tupelo, MS 38803). The Home School Legal Defense Association (P.O. Box 159, Paeonian Springs, VA 22129) defends the legal and political rights of home school families.

Two groups which work actively to preserve Christian values in education, public and private, are the Christian Educators Association International (P.O. Box 50025, Pasadena, CA 91115) and Citizens for Excellence in Education/National Association of Christian Educators (P.O. Box 3200, Costa Mesa, CA 92628).

This general survey of conservative and Christian political organizations is by no means complete. Many others exist, particularly at the state and local levels. And a nationwide organization might be very effective in one state and not particularly effective in another. You will have to evaluate what organizations are most effective in your state and locality, and work with those.

You will also want to evaluate which organization is best suited to your temperament, needs, and interests. Do you desire to concentrate on one issue, like right to life or free enterprise, or do you desire to work on conservative causes generally? In deciding where to focus your energy, you might ask yourself the following questions: Where does there seem to be the greatest need? What issue "grips" me the most? Where do I have the most interest? In which field do I have the most training, experience, knowledge, contacts, or credibility? If you are a doctor or nurse, you might want to concentrate upon health care reform. If you are a small businessman, you might work to defend the free enterprise system. As a teacher or parent you might work for the improvement of education. As a veteran you might be most interested in military issues. You will have to decide in what part of the vineyard the Lord is calling you to labor.

The Church

As we have previously seen, God has established two kingdoms, church and state, to govern man. The believer is a citizen of both kingdoms, with responsibilities toward each, and the link between the two kingdoms. Christians exercise their civic responsibilities primarily as individual citizens rather than as a church body, but the church has responsibilities to the state just as the state has responsibilities toward the church.

The state has a duty to protect the church so that the Word may be preached and heard and so Christians and others will be free to exercise their religious convictions. The state has a duty to give the church the same police protection, fire protection, etc., that it gives to everyone else.

The church has duties to the state as well. The church's first duty to the state is to maintain the moral tone of society, for without morality a free republic is impossible. George Washington said it well in his Farewell Address:

> Of all the dispositions and habits which lead to political prosperity, Religion and Morality are indispensable supports. In vain would that man claim the tribute of Patriotism, who should labor to subvert these great pillars of human happiness, these firmest props of the duties of Men and Citizens. The mere Politician, equally with the pious man, ought to respect and cherish them. A volume could not trace all their

connections with private and public felicity. Let it simply be asked, where is the security for property, for reputation, for life, if the sense of religious obligation desert the oaths which are the instrument of investigation in Courts of Justice? And let us with caution indulge the supposition that morality can be maintained without religion. Whatever may be conceded to the influence of refined education on minds of peculiar structure, religion and experience both forbid us to expect that national morality can prevail in exclusion of religious principle.

Shortly thereafter, a group of twenty-five clergymen wrote to Washington commending him for his nearly half-century of public service and for the observations about religion in his farewell address. Washington responded by thanking them for their letter, and then declared that "Religion and Morality are the essential pillars of civil society." On another occasion, writing to the Dutch Reformed Church in 1789, he observed that "while just government protects all in their religious rights, true religion affords to government its surest support."

Washington's point is that political freedom is possible only in a disciplined, moral society. The sinful nature of man needs restraint, and if people cannot restrain themselves, government must restrain them. Without moral restraint, then, freedom is impossible. But man does not have the capacity for such moral virtue within himself, so moral virtue must come from another source—religion, which term the founding fathers usually used interchangeably with Christianity. His vice-president, John Adams, echoed the same sentiment: "Our constitution was made only for a moral and religious people. It is wholly inadequate for the government of any other." The church, then, sets the moral tone for society as a whole.

The second duty of the church is to preach the gospel of Jesus Christ. Through the gospel God imparts forgiveness of sins and eternal life for the believer. But the state also benefits from the preaching of the Word, for as people's lives are changed, they become better citizens and better members of society. Even men like Franklin and Jefferson, who probably were not orthodox believers in Christianity, recognized the societal value of the church and the gospel in changing people's lives. During the great religious revival known as the First Great Awakening in the 1740s, Ben Franklin befriended the evangelist George Whitefield, contributed large sums of money to his evangelistic efforts, and did his printing for him free of charge, even though he probably never fully accepted Whitefield's theology, because he believed Whitefield's preaching was changing people's lives and making America a better place in which to live. As he observed about Whitefield's preaching in his autobiography, "It was wonderful to see the change soon made in the manners of our inhabitants."

A third responsibility of the church is to teach biblical principles of government. As we have seen before, the Bible speaks extensively of civil government, and leading church theologians throughout history, including Augustine, Aquinas, Luther, and Calvin, have written in great detail about the two kingdoms of church and state and our duties to each. In the 1700s, as elections approached, pastors commonly preached "election sermons" in which they explained the Christian's duty to civil government and exhorted their followers to do their duty as citizens.

Occasionally we hear a preacher say, "I don't preach about politics; I only preach the Bible." He really means "I only preach part of the Bible." For the Bible speaks about civil government and the issues of the day, and the pastor who refuses to address those issues is not preaching the whole counsel of God.

The famous French jurist and political philosopher, Alexis de Tocqueville toured America in the 1830s and wrote the classic work *Democracy in America*. There he made an interesting observation:

> Religion in America takes no direct part in the government of society, but it must be regarded as the first of their political institutions; for if it does not impart a taste for freedom, it facilitates the use of it. Indeed, it is in this same point of view that the inhabitants of the United States themselves look upon religious belief. I do not know whether all Americans have a sincere faith in their religion—for who can search the human heart?—but I am certain that they hold it to be indispensable to the maintenance of their political institutions.

The church should be the divine institution which teaches the basic biblical principles of civil government, where basic civic duties are learned, where biblical principles of economics, social responsibility, war and military service, crime and punishment, obedience and disobedience, and the value of human life are pondered and articulated.

I do not believe the church should be extensively involved in political activism. The church should teach biblical principles of government, duties toward government (including voter registration), and issues concerning government. Individual Christian citizens who have learned biblical principles in the church can then go forth into society and articulate those principles and help implement them.

As a fourth duty which is related to the third, the church should call civil society to repentance for moral evils. The church has done so in the past. For too long the church was apathetic about slavery, but finally the church awakened and led the drive for abolition. The church needs to call the nation to repentance on sins such as abortion, injustice, and acceptance of homosexuality.

In so doing we may be accused of legislating morality. But all law ultimately has a moral base, for all law is the enactment of certain values which have their roots in religious belief. Our legal system was founded on Judeo-Christian values, and as we depart from those values we will incur God's judgment and reap the consequences of our own folly.

A fifth duty of the church is Christian charity. By feeding the poor in emergency situations and helping to counsel and train people for jobs, the church can do much to alleviate poverty. In fact, if the church had done more in this area, many government programs might have been averted.

The Issues: Current Priorities

Space does not permit a detailed exegesis of the biblical position on each key issue facing Americans today, or a detailed scholarly discussion of the facts on each. I have articulated these more fully in *God and Caesar: Christian Faith and Political Action* (Wheaton, Illinois: Crossway, 1984, 1992), and the many sources cited above can help you study these issues further. But in this brief space I would like to survey some of the key issues facing us today and outline a few priorities for action.

Too often conservative Christians react rather than act. We wait for others to propose unacceptable changes and solutions and then fight defensively against them, rather than proposing constructive policies of our own. And we do so on a piecemeal basis, fighting a proposed policy here and there, but without any visible comprehensive plan. We need to take the offensive, in a constructive way, proposing solutions of our own. While we have some excellent conservative thinktanks doing this on the national level, we need more such foundations to address state and local problems. Certainly each state could use its version of the Heritage Foundation, the Cato Institute, or the Hoover Institute.

Let us now shape some priorities on a few broad issues facing us today:

Religious Freedom

We should be thankful that Christians have more freedom to preach the Word of God and practice their religious beliefs in America than in most countries. The truth is that while conflicts between church and state do occur, we in this country don't know what real persecution is—yet.

But the suppression of liberty usually begins with small infringements which set the precedent for ever greater infringements. For this reason we must guard our religious liberty carefully and vigilantly. And we need not hesitate to defend our religious liberties in court if necessary. On at least four occasions Paul claimed his rights as a Roman citizen and as a Jew (Acts 16:23-39; 21:39-40; 22:25-30; 25:9-11). Note, however, that Paul claimed his rights not for personal gain but rather to gain a hearing for the Word of God.

Free exercise of religion is in jeopardy today. In *Wisconsin v. Yoder* (1972), the Supreme Court ruled that free exercise of religion is a fundamental right, and that the state can infringe upon that right only upon showing a compelling state interest that cannot be achieved by less restrictive means. But in *Smith v. Oregon* (1988), the Supreme Court ruled that the compelling interest/less restrictive means test applies only to state regulations that are directly aimed at religion; regulations that only incidentally affect religion can be justified by merely showing a rational relationship to a legitimate state purpose.

This substantially weakens the protection of the free exercise clause. For very few regulations are directly aimed at religion; the vast majority, like zoning laws, employment laws, teacher certification laws, etc., affect society as a whole and the church or Christian citizen is simply caught up in the general net.

Note, also, that this limitation began with a rather innocuous case. *Smith v. Oregon* involved an Oregon statute prohibiting the use of drugs; the Native American Church claimed the law violated their free exercise rights because they use peyote (a mild hallucinogen similar to marijuana) as part of their religious rituals. Not many Christians would want to defend drug use; yet the precedent set by this case has endangered the free exercise of religion for all of us. The Religious Freedom Restoration Act currently pending in Congress, which is designed to restore the compelling interest/less restrictive means test to all matters involving federal funds, deserves serious consideration.

Freedom of religious expression in the public arena needs to be safeguarded. The American Civil Liberties Union and similar groups seem to believe religious expression should be more restricted in public than other forms of expression, because of the establishment clause of the First Amendment. This certainly is not what the framers of the First Amendment had in mind. As Joseph Story, Harvard law professor and Supreme Court justice, wrote in the leading exposition of constitutional law of the 1800s, *Commentaries on the Constitution* (1833),

> Probably at the time of the adoption of the Constitution, and of the amendment to it now under consideration, the general, if not the universal sentiment was, that Christianity ought to receive encouragement from the state, so far as was not incompatible with the private rights of conscience and the freedom of religious worship. An attempt to level all religions, and to make it a matter of state policy to hold all in utter indifference, would have created universal disapprobation, if not universal indignation.

Certainly the framers intended that Christians and other religious believers should have at least as much freedom to express themselves in the public arena as does anyone else. Law foundations mentioned above, like the Christian Legal Society, the Rutherford Institute, and the National Legal Foundation, deserve our financial support as they defend Christian liberties in the courts. And Christians who are looking for a profession in which they can make an impact for Christian values, might seriously consider the study of law.

Education

Education is a primary battleground in the war of ideas. Humanist leader John Dumphey wrote in *The Humanist* magazine, January/February 1983,

> I am convinced that the battle for humankind's future must be waged and won in the public school classroom by teachers who correctly perceive their role as the proselytizers of a new faith: a religion of humanity that recognizes and respects of what theologians call divinity in every human being. These teachers must embody the same selfless dedication as the most rabid fundamentalist preacher, for they will be ministers of another servant, utilizing a classroom instead of a pulpit to convey humanist values in whatever subjects they teach regardless of the educational level—preschool daycare or large state university. The classroom must and will become an arena of conflict between the old and the new—the rotting corpse of Christianity together with all its adjacent evils and misery and the new faith of humanism resplendent in its promise of a world in which the never-realized Christian ideal of "love thy neighbor" will finally be achieved.

The opponents of Christianity could not be more clear. Not only have they declared all-out war against Christianity, they have delineated the public school system as the primary battlefield.

We must therefore be prepared with a plan of attack for education. We must not content ourselves with merely responding to attacks upon our values; we must work for an educational system in which our values are treated fairly. I suggest the following priority points:

(1) Education needs proper funding. Whether or not we ourselves utilize the public schools for our children, children who attend public schools deserve a good education.

(2) Education is best funded and controlled at the local level, with a minimum of federal and even state involvement. Local funding, local control, and local decision making lead to an education system which best reflects the needs and values of families in the local community. Significantly, New Hampshire students are among the highest achievers in the nation, even though state funding of education in New Hampshire is one of the nation's lowest.

(3) In an era when school budgets are already strained to the breaking point, primary emphasis should be upon basic skills rather than unbasic frills. Reading, 'riting, and 'rithmetic should be stressed, and the primary (not necessarily exclusive) tool for teaching reading should be phonics.

(4) Parents should have more input into the educational process and should be given a voice in the selection of texts and curricula. (And parents, when opportunities are provided, you need to volunteer!)

(5) While public schools cannot teach specific church doctrine, there is no reason schools can't teach basic Judeo-Christian values such as honesty, kindness, respect for others, abstinence, patriotism, the value of liberty, the work ethic, etc. Teachers who do so, whether by word or by example, deserve our special commendation and support.

(6) Likewise there is no reason schools cannot teach the facts concerning the Christian beliefs of our founding fathers and the ways Christianity shaped our culture and form of government. The truth or falsity of Christian teaching is a matter of doctrinal disagreement; the

founders' belief in Christianity and practice of Christianity is established historical fact. The attempt to delete these facts from our history texts is nothing but distortion and censorship and should be exposed for what it is.

(7) The right of equal access of religious groups to use public facilities, guaranteed by the First Amendment and further secured by the Equal Access Act of 1984, must be safeguarded at all costs. Student religious groups have the same right to use public school facilities as other student groups; the same principle should apply to outside organizations which desire to use public school facilities for their meetings.

(8) Evolution is more than a scientific model of origins; it is a philosophical worldview with significant religious implications. The dogmatic and exclusive teaching of evolution in public schools is unfair to other religious worldviews. Contrary to popular opinion, the Supreme Court in *Edwards v. Aguillard* (1987) did not prohibit all teaching of creation-science; they simply ruled that that particular Louisiana law was unconstitutional because it lacked a secular purpose. Language in the majority opinion indicated that in other circumstances a two-model approach might be permissible. States, local school boards, and individual teachers should not be afraid to adopt a two-model approach, despite threats and intimidation from the ACLU and similar groups. In doing so they should seek help from one or more of the legal foundations mentioned above.

How about combining the ideas of equal access and teaching creation-science, and establishing a Creation Club, or an Origins Club, in your public high school?

(9) Competition generally improves quality, but there is little competition if parents do not have any choice in education. "Open transfer" policies, by which parents can choose to send their children to schools other than the one they are assigned to, enable parents to choose the school that best meets their children's needs, foster

competition among public schools to meet those parents' needs, and should thus improve overall educational quality. It is indeed strange that some who yell so stridently for choice in other areas of policy, oppose giving parents a choice in their children's education.

(10) Parents who prefer private or home education for their children should be free to make that choice with a minimum of government intrusion. Whether private and home schools should receive government help such as vouchers or tax credits is more problematic. On the one hand it seems unfair that parents who pay taxes to support the public schools should have to provide alternative education entirely at their own expense, especially when the public schools have in some cases constructively evicted them by teaching contrary to their religious beliefs. On the other hand, government aid leads to government control, and to be distinctive private schools need to keep their independence.

(11) The custom of praying at graduation services lends dignity, solemnity, and reverence to this rite of passage and should be preserved. Again, contrary to popular opinion the Supreme Court did not rule in *Lee v. Weisman* (1992) that all prayer at graduation was unconstitutional. If school officials distance themselves from religious activity and issue proper disclaimers, such prayer would probably be upheld.

(12) Regardless of whether we send our own children to public schools, we should view the public school system as a mission field. Christian teachers and administrators can have a powerful witness in the public schools.

The Right to Life

By a 5-4 majority the Supreme Court in *Planned Parenthood v. Casey* (1992) ruled that while states can regulate abortion more than was previously thought, they cannot utterly prohibit abortion at least at the present time.

The Court's inability to reach a consensus or clear

resolution of this issue probably reflects the uncertainty of society itself. While clear majorities of the American people say they believe the unborn child is a living human being and that they are morally opposed to abortion in most instances, there is no clear consensus that all abortion should be banned at the present time. With the uncertainty that exists today, the following priorities should be considered:

(1) We need to redouble our efforts to educate people about the evil of abortion and the humanity of the unborn child. Films like *The Silent Scream* that show the horror of an unborn child screaming as he is killed in the womb should be shown in churches, civic groups, and when possible on television. It is ugly and revolting, but so were the death camps at Auschwitz and Dachau. Remember, it took generations for Western society to reach a consensus that slavery is wrong, but we finally arrived, and the church led the way.

(2) The Freedom of Choice Act, by which Congress would enact into federal law the right to abortion on demand at any stage of pregnancy, would deny freedom of choice to unborn babies or to states to choose their own abortion policies. We need to resist this bill at all costs.

(3) While Americans may not be willing at present to enact laws prohibiting abortion entirely, laws prohibiting abortion except for rape or incest or to save the life of the mother might receive majority support and might be upheld by the courts. For some of us this is a compromise that is not entirely satisfactory, for it is wrong to execute an innocent child for the sin of his or her parent (Deut. 24:16). But politics involves resolving competing interests, and in the political arena usually no one gets everything he wants. If you have done everything you can in working for what you believe is right, it is not compromise to settle for less than you really want if you are convinced that is the best you can get at the time.

(4) Polls indicate a strong majority of the population opposes public funding of abortion. With strained budgets today, particularly in the field of health care, our chances of preventing further government spending to fund abortion should be good.

(5) Polls also indicate a majority favors laws requiring parental notice or parental consent before a minor obtains an abortion. We should work for the enactment of such laws, and they should be upheld as constitutional so long as the law provides that a minor can prove to a judge that she is mature enough to make her own choice.

(6) Laws that require waiting periods for a woman to think over the question of abortion, and that require that she be given certain information about the unborn child and the abortion procedure so she can make an informed decision, should be enacted where they do not already exist.

(7) Laws that require an anesthetic to the unborn child during an abortion should be enacted. Medical evidence demonstrates that the unborn child is capable of feeling pain. The anesthetic proposal places abortion advocates in the difficult position of having to either acknowledge the ability of the child to feel pain, or to argue that the unborn child is entitled to less protection than livestock in the slaughterhouse.

(8) We can work for laws prohibiting insurance companies from covering abortion except as a special rider, so most people aren't forced to subsidize other people's abortions, and for "conscience" laws that allow medical personnel to refuse to participate in abortions without fear of lawsuit or other reprisals.

(9) Laws that facilitate adoption as an alternative to abortion should be encouraged, and we should fully support the work of crisis pregnancy centers.

Remember—the real goal is not enacting legislation; the real goal is saving babies' lives. We still have the power of persuasion, and every abortion dissuaded is a baby saved.

Health Care

The much-publicized health care crisis today is real. But the problem is not so much health care itself— American health care is some of the best in the world. The problem, rather, is paying for it.

Millions of people are without health insurance today. Sometimes this is because they are uninsurable, sometimes because they can't afford it, sometimes because they choose to spend their money on other things. How many times have you said about a proposed purchase, "I can't afford it," when technically you probably could have purchased it but you considered another purchase more important at the time?

Unfortunately, many of the proposed solutions would simply make the problem worse. Socialized medicine has been a failure wherever it has been tried, resulting in doctor shortages, substandard care, long waiting lists for operations, etc. Managed health care leads to black markets and government officials and/or insurance adjustors making decisions as to who gets what care and at what cost; people have died because their insurance companies refused to authorize medical procedures (Ruth Simon, "A Flawed Remedy: Managed Health Care," *Money* [April 1993], pp. 114-26). On the other hand, national health insurance without any controls would cause costs to soar beyond our ability to pay. After all, there would be no incentive for doctors and hospitals to keep costs down at all!

The National Association of the Self-Employed (2121 Precinct Line Road, Hurst, TX 76054, 800-232-NASE), a group of over 320,000 self-employed persons, has a promising alternative: unmanaged health care in which you have freedom of choice of any doctors and any hospitals throughout the world, coverage on the job and coverage for medical procedures up to your policy limit of two million dollars per person, without the "usual, customary and reasonable" limitations and without pre-call or pre-authorization. But an incentive to save money is placed into the system, and it is placed squarely on the customer: He can get the unused portion of his premiums back when he reaches age 65. That's a powerful incentive for him to use his premium money wisely. The NASE is also speaking out for 100 percent deductibility of health insurance premiums for every American.

Government could encourage programs like that of NASE by allowing "medical IRAs," individual retirement accounts by which taxpayers could place a certain amount per year in tax-deductible savings accounts, use those accounts for medical expenses, and keep whatever is left over for their retirement years.

After all the studies have been conducted and all the options have been analyzed, we may well find that the best solutions are found in the good old American free enterprise system.

But is that really so surprising?

Gay Rights

During the 1980s many liberal causes lost momentum, but one notable exception is that of gay rights. Public acceptance of homosexuality seems to have increased substantially during the past decade.

But President Clinton's effort to lift the ban on gays in the military in January 1993 may have been the high point of the homosexual movement. Since January the pendulum seems to have swung the other way. As military personnel have articulated their objections to lifting the ban, the public has come to realize that this is not just another civil rights issue. The fact that homosexuals constitute only about 2 percent of the population but account for 67 percent of all AIDS cases and are disproportionately at risk for many other diseases (including Hepatitis A, B, and C; syphilis; gonorrhea; rectal injury, and others); are more likely to engage in child sexual abuse, alcohol and drug abuse; and experience emotional problems such as anxiety and depression is a stark reminder that moral proscriptions against homosexuality not only have ancient roots but are grounded in sound medical and scientific evidence.

Nor should we allow ourselves to be cowed into submission by specious claims of constitutional rights. The fact is, the Supreme Court ruled in *Bowers v. Hardwick* (1986) that the Constitution does not guarantee a right to engage in homosexual acts and that the states may make homosexual acts illegal.

While homosexuals do not all speak with one voice, the radical gay rights leadership has an agenda that does not stop at mere tolerance. They want nothing less than full acceptance of homosexuality, and ultimately theirs is a rebellion against the very idea that there is such a thing as normality.

The gay rights movement tries to bring itself under the banner of civil rights by claiming theirs is an orientation over which they have no control, that they are "born that way." The fact that so many have left the homosexual lifestyle, either through therapy or through religious conversion, demonstrates that homosexuality is ultimately the result of choices one makes.

For this reason we should oppose efforts to treat homosexuals as a special minority group. We should oppose the enactment of special gay rights ordinances and, where enacted, we should work for their repeal.

And also for this reason, we should always hold out hope to the homosexual. We should emphasize that Christ died for the sins of the homosexual just as He died for the sins of everyone else, that there is hope that they need not be locked into a lifestyle that is in fact a deathstyle, but rather that deliverance and new life is available through proper help, appropriate medical, psychological, biblical-spiritual counselors, the removal of oneself from that environment, and through our Lord and Savior, Jesus Christ.

Defense and Foreign Policy

Even as the ashes of the Communist empire grow cold, we have not learned that a strong defense deters aggression and thus preserves peace. We still live in a world of "wars and rumors of wars."

The Communist bloc is in shambles right now, but it is too soon to write the obituary of Communism. Communism is still firmly in power in the world's most populous nation, the People's Republic of China, and also holds power in other parts of the world such as North Korea, North Vietnam, and Cuba. While communism appears to have lost power in the former U.S.S.R., at least for the present, if the people of those republics become disillusioned with the instability of republican government and free enterprise economics, they could return the hard-line Communists to power. Or, they could turn to a Fascist dictatorship that could be just as menacing.

Meanwhile, the former Soviet arsenal remains and is subject to proliferation through sale or theft. At a time like this, Strategic Defense Initiative, the technology that would provide a global shield protecting us from nuclear attack, is more vital than ever. Most Americans seem unaware that we have no defense against a missile attack; we can retaliate and destroy our enemy, but we are powerless to deflect the attack and prevent our own destruction. The SDI technology that would remedy that situation has now been placed on hold.

And even if the Communist bloc dissolves, other enemies could arise. The increasing militancy of the Muslim nations is a major problem. Fortunately for the West, many of the Muslim nations such as Turkey, Egypt, Pakistan, and Saudi Arabia have been pro-Western; and some of those who are anti-Western, such as Iraq and Iran, have been too busy fighting each other to constitute a threat. But if the Muslim nations were to join together into one coherent bloc, including some of the former Soviet republics that are largely Muslim, they would truly be a world power.

So a strong and modernized military force remains as necessary as ever. But even the most modern weapons systems cannot sustain a nation unless they are manned by a disciplined fighting force. Advocates of lifting the gay ban, take note!

Economics

While space does not permit a detailed discussion of economic policy, sound economics requires a recognition that free enterprise is most consistent with individual liberty and human nature as it is described in the Bible. Man is basically self-interested, and while he will work hard to earn a living for himself and his family, he needs that profit motive to produce. Rousing speeches about working hard to build a Socialist workers' paradise may motivate him for part of an afternoon, but not much longer.

Excessive government regulation of business, and so-called progressive (actually regressive) taxation that encourages mediocrity and discourages hard work, excellence, risk and entrepreneurism, slows down the economy and is counterproductive in the long run. Sound economic policy must be based upon biblical principles of free enterprise and individual freedom.

This does not mean we have no responsibility to the poor. But welfare systems that discourage families from staying together and make it more profitable to collect welfare than to work at a low-paying job, may hurt the poor in the long run by locking them into a demoralizing system. It should never be more profitable for married people to live separately than together; it should never be more profitable for people to live together unmarried than married; and it should never be more profitable to collect welfare than to work at even the most menial job.

If you give a person a fish, you feed him for a day.

If you teach a person how to fish, you feed him for a lifetime. Jobs and job training are far better than welfare in the long run, and voluntary charity is better and more efficient than government programs. Welfare should be a temporary stopgap measure, not a permanent way of life. Admittedly these maxims are simplistic, but they are basic principles upon which sound economic policy can be based.

Environment

Sound environmental policy must flow from a realistic, biblical view of man's relationship to the environment.

The New Age, neo-pagan view that deifies the earth and makes it (or rather, her) an object of worship, leads to stagnation rather than progress.

The Darwinian view that sees man as part of nature and involved in a tooth-and-claw struggle for survival of the fittest provides no basis for caring for the environment. After all, why should we save the spotted owls if Darwin is correct? Based upon his view of natural selection, we are involved in a struggle for survival with the spotted owls. If we kill all the spotted owls, then that proves we are the more fit species, natural selection has prevailed, and the spotted owls deserved to become extinct.

In contrast to both of these views, the biblical view sees man as having been created in the image of God and given dominion over the earth (Gen. 1-2). He has the right to use the resources God has placed under his dominion, but he also has the duty to be a good steward of God's resources and use them wisely. Under this view there is a basis for saving endangered species—preserving the resources God has created.

In the biblical view, man neither competes with nature nor worships nature. Rather, he sees God's handiwork in nature, and he builds a civilization upon nature while preserving nature's beauty and using the natural resources wisely.

Sound ecological practices can and should be based upon this biblical view of man's relationship with nature. We should also be careful of the tendency of modern environmentalists to blame American entrepreneurs for all of the world's environmental problems. The fact is, managed state economies do not do a very good job of preserving the environment either. Economic policies that provide tax breaks for environmental practices, making it in an industry's self-interest to practice sound ecology, will work best in the long run.

Constitutionalism

The fifty-five delegates who gathered at Independence Hall in Philadelphia in 1787 and drafted our Constitution faced a basic question: How do we give government enough power to govern effectively, yet restrain that power so it does not become oppressive and tyrannical, given the true (biblical) nature of man?

James Madison, whom many call the "Father of the Constitution," had studied for the ministry at the College of New Jersey; he stayed a semester after graduation so he could study Hebrew under the Reverend Witherspoon and learn the Old Testament better. He read the Hebrew laws and institutions in the original language, and this undoubtedly influenced his view of law and government. He wrote in the *Federalist No. 51*,

> But what is government itself but the greatest of all reflections on human nature? If men were angels, no government would be necessary. If angels were to govern men, neither external nor internal controls on government would be necessary. In framing a government which is to be administered by men over men, the great difficulty lies in this: You must first enable the government to control the governed; and in the next place, oblige it to control itself.

If the framers had not believed in the sinfulness of human nature, they would not have addressed the problem this way. But knowing that man is as the Bible describes him, they knew government is necessary, and they also knew government must be carefully limited. So they set forth a government of limited, delegated powers, having only those powers that "we the people" delegate to it in the Constitution, and reserving all others to the states and to the people as stated in the Tenth Amendment. They divided government powers between federal and state levels, and they separated those powers among legislative, executive, and judicial branches, providing checks and balances by which each branch limits the power of the others. They also specifically protected certain rights of the individual citizen against government abuse, so that even the majority could not violate the rights of the minority. The framers were not willing to trust unlimited government power to anyone—even the majority of the people!

We have moved a long way from the model of government established by the framers. In too many judicial circles, the original intent of the framers is no longer controlling; rather, the Constitution is to be interpreted according to an evolving standard by which its meaning changes from year to year and generation to generation. Under this principle rights and liberties are no longer secure and protected; they are subject to the changing whims of the court. And the same court that can create new rights not found in the Constitution, like the right to engage in homosexual conduct or the right to an abortion, can just as easily read rights out of the Constitution that the founders thought they had protected, such as free exercise of religion, or liberty of contract, or property rights, or the right to own firearms. And under this evolving standard the power of the judge becomes virtually absolute, because he can make words mean whatever he wants them to mean.

Individual liberties are now only as secure as the courts wish to make them. And states' rights, the very cornerstone of our constitutional system as evidenced by the Tenth Amendment, are virtually nonexistent since the 5-4 *Garcia v. San Antonio Metropolitan Transit Authority* decision of 1985 in which Justice Blackmun ruled that even wages and hours of state and local employees are subject to federal regulation.

To preserve the constitutional system that has made the United States a model of stability, liberty, justice, and prosperity for the world, we need judges who will interpret the Constitution strictly as intended by the framers. We can and should work for selection of such judges at the state and local level, but we especially need such judges on the federal bench.

How do we find such judges? We need to train them in law schools that teach constitutional principles of law in a Judeo-Christian context, including the Thomas Goode Jones School at Faulkner University (5345 Atlanta Highway, Montgomery, AL 36193), or Regent School of Law (Virginia Beach, VA), or Simon Greenleaf School of Law (3855 E. LaPalma Ave., Anaheim, CA 92807), or Campbell University School of Law (P.O. Box 158, Buies Creek, NC 27506). These schools deserve your prayers and support.

But as you may have guessed, we need to elect a president who will appoint such judges, and senators who will vote to confirm them.

A Closing Call to Arms

We are in a winnable war—a war to preserve the biblical principles that made this country great.

If reading this book has filled you with concern about our nation, I urge you not to put the book down until you have firmly decided to act. Before you move on to other activities, and forget about what you have read, please decide firmly that you are going to take some concrete action—register to vote, write a letter to your newspaper or legislator, contact the political party of your choice, join a civic organization, or something comparable—within the next twenty-four hours. And then resolve to follow it up with more. I warn you: It can become addictive! I also urge you to place yourself under the authority of a church that teaches the Word of God in all its ramifications, so you may grow spiritually and doctrinally and have the blessing and encouragement of good Christian fellowship. You will find that Paul was right: "The Word of God is alive and Powerful!" (Heb. 4:12).

Remember Esther, the Persian queen who was asked to risk her life to save her people? When she hesitated, Mordecai exhorted her to act, and asked rhetorically,

> Who knoweth whether thou art come to the kingdom
> for such a time as this? (Esther 4:14)

God desires to use you, just as He chose to use Esther. But to be used of God, you have to first be prepared, get into the public arena and "put on the full armour of God that we may be able to withstand in the evil day, and, having done all, to stand" (Eph. 6:13). I love these stirring words of Teddy Roosevelt:

> It is not the critic who counts; not the man who points out how the strong man stumbled, or where the doer of deeds could have done them better. The credit belongs to the man who is actually in the arena, whose face is marred by dust and sweat and blood; who strives valiantly; who errs and comes short again and again; who knows the great enthusiasms, the great devotions; who spends himself in a worthy cause; who, at the best, knows in the end the triumph of high achievement, and who at the worst, if he fails at least fails while daring greatly, so that his place shall never be with those timid souls who know neither victory nor defeat.

So that is my challenge to you: Be prepared! And get into the arena! For who knoweth whether *thou* art come to the kingdom for such a time as this?

Appendix

Can Dispensationalists and Reconstructionists Work Together? Yes, If They Read Luther!

A Reconstructionist mindset with dispensational theology! That's a strange combination, but an accurate portrayal of the dilemma in which many evangelicals in today's "Christian Right" find themselves.

Trained in dispensational theology, they hold firmly to the premillennial return of Jesus Christ and the pretribulation rapture of the Church; and they believe the covenant God made with Moses applies to Israel, not the Church. As they watch America sink into immorality, secular humanism and paganism, they are attracted to the Reconstructionist attempt to apply biblical law to the nation's problems. But they wonder, "Is this consistent with our theology?"

Almost everywhere I speak throughout the nation, someone asks me, "Dr. Eidsmoe, are you a Reconstructionist?" I answer "No," but with qualifications. If Christian Reconstruction means the belief that the Mosaic law is part of the Mosaic Convenant, is binding upon the Church and/or America today just as it was binding upon Israel during Old Testament times, and that by applying the Mosaic law to our society we are helping to create conditions which will usher in the millennium, then I most emphatically am not a Reconstructionist. But if the term is used with a broad brush to cover everyone who believes there are absolute principles of right and wrong which are found in God's Word and which can and should be applied to our nation and every other nation, then in that broadest sense I suppose the term could be applied to me. But that is not the definition of reconstruction, and I have never called myself a Reconstructionist, though I support many of the social and political goals of Reconstructionists and am willing to work with them to achieve these goals.[1]

As we will see, Dispensationalists and Reconstructionists differ substantially on several central points of theology: eschatology (pre- vs. postmillennial theology), the application of the Mosaic law, and the current status of Israel, to name a few. But they also agree on many points: the sovereignty of the Triune God, the inspirations and inerrancy of Scripture, the Lordship of Jesus Christ, His substitutionary atonement on the Cross, justification by grace through faith, and in general a conservative lifestyle and conservative political views. Let me add that all of these views are shared by Luther and by traditional Lutherans.

There is no way a treatise of this length can resolve the theological differences that divide Dispensationalists and Reconstructionists. My hope, rather, is that I can provide a framework within which Dispensationalists and Reconstructionists, recognizing their differences, can concentrate upon their points of agreement and work together for common social, political and even theological goals.

And here is my major reason for writing: I sense the coming of a major rift between the Reconstructionist and dispensational camps that could render Christian involvement in government and the political gains we have made over the past decade a nullity. Dispensationalists are being led to lambast Reconstructionist political activity as unbiblical. Reconstructionists, with the wrath that comes with feeling betrayed by one whom you thought was your ally, respond by calling their dispensational brethren lethargic, defeatist, and "pessimillennial." I hope that by establishing this framework I may help to avoid a major split in the conservative evangelical community along dispensational/reconstruction lines, a split that could hamstring and paralyze evangelical involvement in politics.

Finally, I believe Luther's writings can provide an important part of the framework. And if, through this writing, more traditional Lutherans can be awakened from their lethargy and motivated to action, that would be an added benefit.

So that adherents of the two theological systems can better understand each other, let's begin with an explanation of both systems.

Dispensationalism

Dispensationalism can perhaps best be described as a theological system which holds that God deals differently, though always on the basis of grace, with different peoples and at different times. Central to dispensational theology, therefore, is a perpetual distinction between Israel and the Church. In the Old Testament God made certain promises to Israel through the Abrahamic Covenant and the Mosaic Covenant. And even though Israel has repeatedly broken those covenants by sin and apostasy, God will remain faithful to His Word and will fulfill His convenants with Israel. Israel's unfaithfulness merely delays the fulfillment of God's promises; it does not mean those promises are terminated or nullified.

For example, God promised that Israel would possess the Promised Land as a perpetual inheritance, and He promised Israel eternal blessing and a special place among the nations. Because of Israel's apostasy, God has allowed that nation to be dispersed among the nations of the world, and He has allowed them to be the subjects of persecution. But ultimately God will fulfill His promises. One day Israel will be regathered into the Promised Land, and Israel will return to God. Dispensationalists believe this will happen during or just before a seven-year period known in Scripture as the Tribulation, after which Christ will return, defeat His enemies at the Battle of Armageddon, and establish the Millennium, His thousand-year reign on earth, during which Israel will enjoy peace, prosperity, divine favor, and a special place among the nations.[2]

The point is this: Dispensationalists insist that these promises were made to Israel, not the Church, and not to

America—and in dispensational theology there is a perpetual distinction between Israel and the Church. Therefore these promises will be fulfilled to Israel, not to the Church and not to America.

Now, the Mosaic law of the Old Testament is part of the Mosaic Covenant. Under the Mosaic Covenant, Israel promised to keep and obey the Mosaic law. That law was given to Israel, and that promise is binding upon Israel. The Mosaic law was not necessarily given to the Church, or to America, and it is therefore not necessarily binding upon, or even applicable to or appropriate for, the Church or America.

Many Dispensationalists therefore see little reason to apply Old Testament passages to modern America, or to bring America in line with the "law of God" as revealed in the Mosaic Covenant. They have great difficulty with any suggestion that America is somehow a "chosen" or "special" nation today. America to them has no special convenant relationship with God; rather, America is a nation just like any other. Consequently, the notion that America is secular or pluralistic does not bother them nearly as much as it bothers Reconstructionists.

Another central feature of Dispensationalist thought is premillennial eschatology. Eschatology, of course, is the study of the last days. Premillennialists believe there will be a literal one-thousand year reign of Jesus Christ on the earth. The term "premillennial" stems from their belief that, before the millennium, Jesus Christ will personally return to the earth at the Battle of Armageddon, defeat His enemies and bind them in the pit, and establish His millennial rule. Perhaps it should be noted here that while all Dispensationalists are premillennial, not all premillennialists are dispensational.

Before Armageddon and the millennium, there will be a turbulent seven-year period known in Scripture as the "Tribulation." At some point known as the "Rapture" (from the Latin word *rapere*, meaning to take away), the Church (meaning all believers alive and dead) will be caught up to heaven. Premillennialists do not agree on the point at which the Rapture will take place. Pretribulationists (probably the majority) believe the Rapture will take place before the Tribulation; posttribulationists believe the Rapture will be after the Tribulation and at the same time as Armageddon; Midtribulationists believe it will happen in the middle of that seven-year period; partial rapture advocates believe some Christians will be raptured before the Tribulation while others will be left to go through that period of turmoil. Dispensationalists generally hold the pretribulation Rapture position.

Some question the relevance of such futuristic speculation, likening it to debate over how many angels can dance on the head of a pin. But we should remember that fully 20 percent of the Bible is prophecy. More to the point, one's view of the eschatology affects one's view of history and our role in history. In the dispensational and premillennial view, the world is not getting better; no "golden age" is dawning. Rather things are gradually getting worse, because the "golden age" known as the Millennium will come only after the seven-year Tribulation, the worst period of human history. In this view, the general direction of history is downward, not upward; things are going to get worse, not better.

Partially for this reason, many Dispensationalists are reluctant to become involved in politics or other efforts for social change. Why spend all that effort trying to reform a world that is inevitably heading for destruction anyway?

This idea has even more force if one believes, as Dispensationalists do, that before the Tribulation takes place, all believers will be taken up to be with Christ in heaven in a pretribulation Rapture. Again, why reform a world that is headed for tribulation and destruction, especially if we Christians aren't even going to be here when those events happen? As D. L. Moody is said to have asked, "Why polish the brass rails on a sinking ship?" Better to save a soul here and there, like pulling faggots out of the fire or placing people in lifeboats while the ship sinks, and keep our own lives pure as we wait for our Lord's return.

Dispensational theology is not the unique province of any one denomination. The Plymouth Brethren probably hold to dispensationalism more purely than any other body, but most Baptists are dispensational to some degree. And many of the clergy and especially the laity of most denominations have dispensational tendencies. Partly this is due to the influence of radio ministries that have reached millions, such as Back to the Bible Broadcast and Radio Bible Class, and to the influence of well-known preachers like D. L. Moody. The dispensational interpretation of Scripture is set forth in the popular *Scofield Reference Bible,* the circulation of which has crossed denominational lines. (Growing up in western South Dakota, my mother was raised on the *Scofield Bible* in her Missouri Synod Lutheran home. I have heard even United Methodist ministers complain that their congregations were hooked on the *Scofield Bible!*)

Among the leading centers of dispensationalism today are Dallas Theological Seminary, Grace Theological Seminary, Talbot School of Theology, and Moody Bible Institute. Dr. Lewis Sperry Chafer, first president of Dallas Theological Seminary, articulated dispensational theology in his eight-volume work *Systematic Theology,* published by Dallas Seminary Press. Moody Press of Chicago has published Dallas Theological Seminary professor Charles Ryrie's shorter and very readable book, *Dispensationalism Today.* Dispensational eschatology is perhaps articulated in *Things to Come,* a 633-page work by Dallas professor J. Dwight Pentecost, published by Zondervan of Grand Rapids, Michigan. The political ramifications of dispensationalism are discussed in an October 1985 article in *Moody Monthly* by Dr. Norman Geisler, titled "A Premillennial View of Law and Government."

Reconstruction

The Reconstructionist movement is based largely upon covenant theology. Central to covenant theology is God's covenant with man, a covenant of law and a covenant of grace. Some consider these two covenants; others consider them two aspects of the same covenant.

Unlike dispensational theology which teaches that the covenants are unconditional, covenant theology holds that God's covenants are conditional upon man's obedience.

Since Israel has repeatedly broken the covenant, God has cut Israel off from God's promises, and the Church now stands in Israel's place. The promises God made to Israel in the Mosaic Covenant are being fulfilled, not to the Israel of the Old Testament, but to the New Israel, the Church. This does not mean the Jews today are an accursed people, but it does mean the Jews no longer have any special place in God's plan but rather are just like any other people. A Jew has the same opportunity as any other person to be saved and be part of the Church through faith in Jesus Christ.

But if the Church is the New Israel and the heir to God's promises to Israel under the Mosaic Covenant, it is also the heir to Israel's obligations to God under the Mosaic law. At least two factors make the Mosaic law applicable today.

The first is the concept of the holy commonwealth. Like many of our Puritan founders, Reconstructionists are likely to see all government as based on a covenant between men and God. God gives governmental authority to the people, who in turn covenant together in His presence to form a government. The covenant concept therefore applies not only to the Church and the individual believer but to society as a whole.

Second is postmillennial eschatology. As unimportant as it may seem to some today, eschatology is at the root of the differences between dispensational and Reconstructionist thinking.

Dispensationalists and Reconstructionists both believe in a literal thousand-year period during which God's Kingdom will be established on earth. (Please note, however, that while the founders of modern reconstruction were postmillennial, the movement has grown so dramatically during the past decade that it has absorbed many who do not share the presuppositions of the movement's founders. Some leading Reconstructionists today do not appear to have a clearly defined eschatological position. Several call themselves "optimistic amillennialists," believing there will be no literal thousand-year Millennium but that the present age is gradually getting better. There may even be a few premillennialists who call themselves Reconstructionists, though I am not among them.)

Dispensationalists are premillennial—they believe that prior to the establishment of Christ's millennial rule on earth there will be a seven-year period of Tribulation, at the close of which Christ will return and defeat His enemies at Armageddon and establish His millennial Kingdom.

But Reconstructionists in general are postmillennial—they believe God is working through the Church to bring about those ideal conditions on earth which will be conducive to His millennial rule. Some do not believe in a literal seven-year Tribulation; others believe the Tribulation and Armageddon will take place at the close of the millennium, not at the beginning.

Thus for the Reconstructionist the direction of history is very different. History is moving upward, not downward, as we advance toward the millennium. Christians are involved in every front in battles with the forces of evil, but with God's help we are gradually winning. Ever so slowly, the world is getting better in preparation for the millennium.

For the Dispensationalist it is the opposite. We might win a battle here and there, but in general sin is spreading through the world like a cancer and things are getting worse and worse as we approach the Tribulation during which the Antichrist will rule the earth.

But in the Reconstructionist view, we are winning the battle. And one of the ways we fight and win is to work through the courts and the political process to establish biblical standards of law that are compatible with God's will, God's character, God's Word, and God's reign. In this way, but also in many others, He works through us to advance His Kingdom.

So the Mosaic law is applicable today, at least in part. Reconstructionists agree that the civil and moral aspects of the law apply today, though they might disagree among themselves as to how literally to apply them. For example, the Old Testament clearly teaches that homosexuality is wrong. Few if any of the Reconstructionists would favor the legalization of homosexual acts. But must modern American society execute homosexuals as the Mosaic law commands? And if so, must we use the biblical method of execution (stoning), or would other means (firing squad, the electric chair) be acceptable instead? What about blasphemy, and Sabbath-breaking? If we consider these to be "petty" matters, do we take them less seriously than God does? Reconstructionists wrestle with questions like these, and they do not always come to the same conclusions.

Leading Reconstructionist thinkers today include Dr. R. J. Rushdoony of the Chalcedon Foundation in Vallecito, California. His monumental work, *The Institutes of Biblical Law* (Nutley, N.J.: Craig Press, 1973), is a lengthy but excellent work exceeding nine hundred pages; a second volume has been published, and Dr. Rushdoony is planning a third. Another center of Reconstructionist thought is Dominion Press of Tyler, Texas, headed by Dr. Gary North. His *Dominion Covenant* is a multi-volume work still in production. A third is professor Greg Bahnsen, author of *Theonomy in Christian Ethics* (Phillipsburg, N.J.: Presbyterian and Reformed, 1979) and *By This Standard* (Tyler, Tex.: Institute for Christian Economics, 1985). A fourth is American Vision of Atlanta, Georgia, headed by Dr. Gary DeMar. His works include *God and Government* and *The Reduction of Christianity*, both published by American Vision.

Those looking for an informative and fairly objective analysis of the dispensationalism/reconstruction debate might wish to read *Dominion Theology: Blessing or Curse?* by Dr. Wayne House and Pastor Thomas Ice, both Dispensationalists (Portland: Multnomah, 1988), or *The Debate over Christian Reconstruction* by Dr. Gary DeMar, a Reconstructionist (Ft. Worth: Dominion Press, 1988).

The reader will note that, while I have made clear that I hold the dispensational position, I have not attempted to prove the dispensational position or refute the reconstruction viewpoint. The debate over premillennial and postmillennial theology must be resolved, ultimately, through detailed exegesis of the many passages of Scripture that deal with eschatology. Volumes have been written on this subject, and it clearly requires more space than can be devoted in this treatise. Dr. J. Dwight Pentecost has ably presented the dispensational view of eschatology in *Things to Come*, referred to above, as has Dr. Charles L. Feinberg in *Millennialism: The Two Major Views* (Chicago: Moody, 1936, 1980); setting forth the postmillennial position are David Chilton in *Paradise Restored: An Eschatology of Dominion* (Tyler, Tex.: Reconstruction Press, 1985), and Dr. Loraine Boettner in *The Millennium* (Phillipsburg, N.J.: Presbyterian and Reformed, 1957, 1984). Two books that present a balanced view of the various perspectives are *Contemporary Options in Eschatology: A Study of the Millennium* by Millard J. Erickson (Grand Rapids: Baker, 1977, 1980); and *A Philosophy of the Second Advent* by Howard A. Redmond (Milford, Mich.: Mott Media, 1985).

Rather than arguing for a particular position, the purpose of this treatise is to enable Dispensationalists and Reconstructionists, and all those caught in the middle, to understand both positions, respect their differences, and find a way to work together in areas of agreement.

The Conflict Over Political Involvement

In *The Biblical Philosophy of History*, Dr. Rushdoony sounds a clarion call for a full-scale crusade to establish biblical values:

> Man must exercise dominion in the name of God, and in knowledge, righteousness, and holiness. Education must be Christian, because all non-Christian education is committed to beliefs which are either implicitly or explicitly at war with the Christian faith. Christian education must also be philosophically informed and epistemologically self-conscious; it cannot be Christian unless it re-thinks every area of study in terms of a consistent and systematic Biblical faith.

> The world, moreover, cannot be surrendered to Satan. It is God's world and must be brought under God's law, politically, economically, and in every other way possible.

> The enlightenment, by its savage and long standing attack on Biblical faith, has brought about a long retreat of Christianity from a full-orbed faith to a kind of last-ditch battle centering around the

doctrines of salvation and of the infallible Scripture. The time has come for a full-scale offense, and it has indeed begun, to bring every area of thought into captivity to Christ, to establish the whole counsel of God and every implication of His infallible word.[3]

In keeping with this call to arms, Reconstructionists have articulated scholarly position papers detailing biblical positions on issues such as interest rates, the coining of money, economic systems, criminal justice, capital punishment, foreign policy, national defense, abortion, and many other subjects. In so doing they have caused many Christians to rethink social issues in the light of biblical norms and standards.

Dispensationalists, who also treasure the Bible as God's Word and look forward to His millennial reign, cannot help but be stirred by the Reconstructionist call to arms. But at the same time, many sense, sometimes rather vaguely, that there is something about restructuring society along biblical lines that is somehow inconsistent with dispensational theology. As a result, many look upon the Reconstructionist agenda with mixed emotions.

In fact, it would be fair to say that many, perhaps most, Christian Right evangelicals have a Reconstructionist mindset with dispensational theology; they share the Reconstructionist vision but with dispensational reservation. The Rev. Jerry Falwell is a Dispensationalist, but when he preaches about Christianity and government he often sounds like a Reconstructionist. Dr. Francis Schaeffer's *A Christian Manifesto* sounds like a Reconstructionist manifesto, yet Dr. Schaeffer was premillennial. Is there a tension between these positions? If so, can it be resolved?

One can see how these differing theologies can affect one's view of political action. If you believe you are working, with God's help, to bring about God's Kingdom on earth by bringing society into subjection to God's laws, and that while you face stiff opposition you are moving upward to inevitable victory with God's help, you obviously have strong motivation to be involved. But if you believe the world is headed for destruction, that the forces of Antichrist are gradually taking over the earth, and that the most we can expect is a minor victory here and there in a rear-guard action as we wait to be raptured up to heaven, then the motivation for political involvement or social reform is much less clear. Again, as D. L. Moody asked, why polish the brass rails on a sinking ship?

And as Reconstructionists earnestly speak of applying biblical law to our society, Dispensationalists are uneasy. "Certainly we don't want to seem like we're against the Bible," they say to themselves. "But is it really supposed to be applied this way? The Mosaic law was for Israel, this is the Church age, a dispensation of grace. Is this really 'rightly dividing the Word of Truth?'" Dr. Norman Geisler, formerly of Dallas Theological Seminary and now of Liberty University, argues that nations should be governed by the law of nature that comes from God, but are not bound by biblical law.[4]

Likewise, Dispensationalists are skeptical of efforts to bring America back to its "Christian foundations." America is not a modern-day Israel in the Dispensationalist view; it is not, strictly speaking, a "Christian nation" and never was.

Nevertheless, Dispensationalists and Reconstructionists do have certain points in common. Both are committed to evangelical Christianity, as was Martin Luther. Both believe the Bible is the inspired and inerrant Word of God and interpret it more or less literally, as did Luther. Both believe salvation is by grace through faith, as did Luther. And both are essentially conservative in their social and political outlook, as was Luther in his day.

The points of disagreement between dispensationalism and reconstruction are significant and deserve serious discussion. But they need not cause a permanent rift.

Unfortunately, right now dispensationalism and reconstruction are on a collision course. Some Dispensationalists accuse Reconstructionists of seeking to bring in the kingdom through their own efforts, and charge that in that respect Reconstructionists are tools of the New Age conspiracy to establish a heaven on earth. Reconstructionists counter that Dispensationalists, by discouraging Christians from political involvement, are advancing humanism and the New Age movement by creating a political vacuum which Humanists and New Agers gladly fill. A leading evangelical magazine has suggested that the debate over Christian reconstruction is likely to be the "hottest" issue facing evangelicals in the 1990s.

Can this conflict be avoided? I believe it can. I believe a framework of commonly-held positions exists on which Dispensationalists and Reconstructionists, without compromising their convictions, can respect each other's positions and work together for common goals. I believe that framework can be found in the biblical and systematic theology of Martin Luther.

A Framework for Cooperation

(1) The Two Kingdoms

Luther believed God has established two kingdoms to rule over men, the church and the state. The church has authority over only believers and is not authorized to use force to accomplish its objectives. (This does not mean believers may not serve in the military or act as policemen, but when they do so they are serving God as ministers of the state, not the church.) The state has authority over believers and unbelievers alike, and is authorized to use force to accomplish its objective of restraining sin. The believer, being subject to both kingdoms, constitutes the earthly link between the two. Calvin emphasized a two kingdoms concept similar to Luther's but Calvin went further than Luther in stressing the responsibility of the state to aid the church in spreading the gospel.

The two kingdoms concept has its roots in the Old Testament, where the kings always came out of the tribe of Judah and the priests always came out of the tribe of Levi. Governmental authority and religious authority are separate offices with separate jurisdictions, but both derive their authority from God.

The two kingdoms concept is also consistent with the religion clauses of the First Amendment to the U.S. Constitution, properly understood, which says, "Congress shall make no law respecting an establishment of religion, or prohibiting the free exercise thereof." The radical notion of absolute separation of church and state is neither biblical nor in accord with the First Amendment as understood by its framers.[5]

(2) A Christian Nation?

Is America a "Christian nation"? That depends on the meaning of the term. If by "Christian nation" we mean a nation in which everyone is a born-again believer, or in which non-Christians are unwelcome or second-class citizens, then the answer is no, the United States is not a Christian nation.

Using the term in this way, Luther said there could never be a Christian nation because in every society most people are unregenerate:

> First take heed and fill the world with real Christians before ruling it in a Christian and evangelical manner. This you will never accomplish; for the world and the masses are and always will be unchristian, although they are all baptized and are nominally Christians. Christians, however, are few and far between, as the saying is. Therefore it is out of the question that there should be a common Christian government over the whole world, nay even over one land or company of people, since the wicked always outnumber the good. Hence a man who would venture to govern an entire country or the world with the Gospel would be like a shepherd who should place in one fold wolves, lions, eagles, and sheep together and let them freely mingle with one another and say, Help yourselves, and be good and peaceful among yourselves; the fold is open, and there is plenty of food; have no fear of dogs and clubs. The sheep, forsooth, would keep the peace and would allow themselves to be fed and governed in peace, but they would not live long; nor would any beast keep from molesting another.
>
> For this reason these two kingdoms must be sharply distinguished, and both be permitted to remain;

the one to produce piety, the other to bring about external peace and prevent evil deeds; neither is sufficient in the world without the other.[6]

But the term may be used in a different way, to refer to the fundamental values on which the nation is based. The fact that the Declaration of Independence repeatedly refers to God and that the Constitution closes with the words "in the Year of our Lord 1787," coupled with Judeo-Christian principles which underlie these documents such as the higher law of God, the dignity and worth of the individual person, human equality, God-given human rights, government by consent of the governed, and the need to limit and separate governmental power because of the sinful nature of man, is evidence of these Christian foundations.

Those who seek to convert this nation into a secular state use the First Amendment as their primary tool, but to do so they must debunk the "myth" that the founding fathers were Christians. It is therefore not surprising to read secular writers who claim the founding fathers were Deists and skeptics, but it is most disturbing when Christian leaders voice the same "facts" without checking the sources. As one who has studied the founding fathers intensely, I can say flatly that these writers don't know what they're talking about!

In my 415-page book *Christianity and the Constitution* (Grand Rapids: Baker Book House, 1987, 1988), I demonstrate from the founders' own writings that, with few exceptions, they were raised in Christian homes, were taught at home and in Christian schools, studied the Bible at length and quoted it more frequently than any other source, were active church members, and professed belief in the basic doctrines of Christianity. Even those few who probably were not Christians, like Franklin and Jefferson, held a Christian world view and Christian values and respected the influence of Christianity upon the nation.

I believe America can be called a Christian nation, but since that term has several possible meanings and is capable of being misinterpreted, I prefer to say America is a nation based on Christian values—or Judeo-Christian values, if you prefer. This does not mean America is the new Israel, or that America necessarily has a special relationship with God. Dispensationalists do not compromise their principles by recognizing America's Christian foundations. Rather, to refuse to do so is to refuse to face historical reality.

(3) Christians in Politics

Christians have responsibilities to the church and responsibilities to the state. In Luther's view, Christians should not shirk their responsibilities to civil government by retreating from the political arena and developing a ghetto mentality, as did some in that day whom Luther labeled "enthusiasts" and "fanatics." The ideal ruler, according to Luther, is the godly Christian prince. As Luther said,

> A prince must act also in a Christian way toward his God, that is, he must subject himself to Him in entire confidence and pray for wisdom to rule well, as Solomon did. . . . [A] prince's duty is fourfold: First, that toward God consists in true confidence and in sincere prayer; second, that toward his subject consists in love and Christian service; third, that toward his counselors and rulers consists in an open mind and unfettered judgment; fourth, that toward evil doers consists in proper zeal and firmness. Then his state is right, outwardly and inwardly, pleasing to God and to the people. But he must expect much envy and sorrow—the cross will soon rest on the shoulders of such a ruler.[7]

Luther's portrayal of the godly Christian prince is in full accord with Proverbs 29:2: "When the righteous are in authority, the people rejoice: but when the wicked beareth rule, the people mourn."

Many Dispensationalists are uneasy about political activism because, in their view, the Reconstructionists are involved in politics as a means of bringing about the Kingdom of God. Dispensationalists are convinced that the kingdom will not come through human effort to make the world better but rather through the Lord Jesus Christ Himself upon His return at Armageddon. Before that time there will be a seven-year Tribulation during which the Antichrist shall rule the earth. The world is going to get a lot worse before it gets better. In the view of some Dispensationalists, Reconstructionist political efforts to make the world better in preparation for Christ's return are at best futile and possibly dangerous.

But other sound biblical reasons exist for political activism. Our Lord said, "Occupy till I come" (Luke 19:13). The issue is not victory or defeat—and in the dispensational view we are likely to face more defeats than victories as the cancer of sin spreads throughout the earth. The issue is being faithful to God and His standards of righteousness. As our Lord said to the church at Sardis, "Be watchful, and strengthen the things which remain, that are ready to die" (Rev. 3:2). I believe this has a secondary application to society, and that even if we live in a decaying world, we should strengthen the things that remain.

Consider the men and women in the Bible who were active in politics, starting with Israel's kings and judges. Outside the Israelite theocracy, Daniel was prime minister in Babylon and later in Persia. Joseph was prime minister of Egypt. Nehemiah was a trusted advisor of the King of Persia, and Esther was Queen of Persia. In the New Testament we read of Joseph of Arimathea and Nicodemus, members of the Jewish Sanhedrin, a religious, political and legal governing body. In the Epistle to the Romans, probably written from Corinth, Paul brings greetings from "Erastus the chamberlain" (Rom. 16:23). A chamberlain was a city treasurer, a highly political position in a city the size of Corinth. Here is a prominent Corinthian politician who is so involved in the church that Paul brings greetings from him to Christians in the city of Rome. In the Epistle to the Philippians, probably written from Rome, Paul says, "All the saints greet you, chiefly they that are of Caesar's household" (Phil. 4:22). The word "household" [*oikonomea*] may refer to Caesar's relatives; more likely it refers to the

Roman civil service. Again we see politically prominent
men who are so involved in the Roman church that Paul
brings greetings from them in Scripture to the Christians
at Philippi.

Why polish the brass rails on a sinking ship? Because
all ships are going to sink eventually, unless they end up
on dry dock. But they may have a long and useful life
ahead of them, and we should keep them shipshape for as
long as they last.

The same is true of nations. We do not know the hour
of the Lord's return. He said He is coming soon, but in
God's timing a thousand years are as a day (Ps. 90:4). His
return may be during our lifetime or it may be countless
centuries away. During this time there will be good periods
and bad, worldwide and particularly in specific nations
and communities. The overall trend is downhill as the
cancer of sin, but it is not a steady decline. The 1700s and
1800s were among the best periods of history, in terms of
both human happiness and advancement of the gospel.

A leading dispensational writer recently told me Christians should be looking for the Lord's return rather than
immersing themselves in politics. In response, I told him
a story of two bridegrooms. One told his bride, "I am
going away. I will return, but I can't say when. While I am
gone, I want you to quit your job, leave your home and
family, sell your property, and wait on a hilltop for my
return."

The other told his bride, "I am going away. I will
return, but I can't tell you when. While I am gone, take
good care of your home and family. Work hard at your
job, and stay in good health. Be involved in your community, and when you least expect it, I will return."

Now, which bridegroom sounds more like our Lord,
who said, "Occupy till I come"? My friend had to agree it
was the second.

It is said that someone asked Martin Luther, "If you
knew for certain that Christ was coming this afternoon,
what would you do this morning?" Luther's answer was
short but full of meaning: "I'd plant a tree."

(4) The Kingdom of God

Reconstructionists think of their involvement in politics and culture as one of many means of advancing the kingdom of God. Hearing the term *kingdom*, many Dispensationalists think of the millennium. They know human effort can't bring in the millennium, so they wonder whose kingdom the Reconstructionists are bringing in. And it sounds like man trying to save himself through his own works.

First, the charge that Reconstructionists are relying upon works rather than grace is erroneous in my view. They believe salvation is by grace through faith, secured for us by Christ's atoning death on the Cross. And the charge that working to prepare the world for Christ's rule is reliance upon works rather than grace is no more justified than accusing Dispensationalists of believing that preaching the gospel consists of men saving other men. Both involve God working through men to accomplish His objectives, whether the salvation of an individual soul or the transformation of the world.

Let us look at the term *kingdom*. The term is used in many ways in Scripture. Sometimes it refers to the millennium, sometimes it refers to heaven. But Jesus also told us that the kingdom is at hand (Matt. 3:2, 4:17); that the kingdom is come unto you (Matt. 12:28); that the kingdom has come (Mark 9:1); and that the kingdom is within us (Luke 17:21). Clearly the term *kingdom* is not used in Scripture exclusively for the millennium.

Leading dispensational writers have recognized the broad use of the term *kingdom*. Dr. Lewis Sperry Chafer discusses the many uses of the term and says,

> Two specific realms are in view as the doctrine of kingdom receives consideration:
>
> 1. THE KINGDOM OF GOD, which includes all intelligences in heaven or on earth who are willingly subject to God.
>
> 2. THE KINGDOM OF HEAVEN, which embraces any sort of empire that God may have on earth at a given time.[8]

Dr. John F. Walvoord, President Emeritus of Dallas Theological Seminary and a leading dispensational theologian, writes of the sphere of the kingdom and concludes: "It is, therefore, an error to limit His teaching to making all His kingdom messages apply to the millennial period alone. On the other hand, it is equally erroneous to limit His teaching to a spiritual kingdom to be fulfilled before His second advent."[9]

Dr. J. Dwight Pentecost, whose *Things to Come* is probably the leading dispensational work on eschatology, discusses at length the various uses of the kingdom: the eternal kingdom characterized by timelessness, universality, providence, and miracle; the theocratic kingdom from Eden throughout the ages; the kingdom program in the New Testament; the kingdom program in the present age; and the Millennium.[10] And C. I. Scofield, whose *Scofield Reference Bible* has probably reached more people than any other single source of dispensational teaching, recognizes the various aspects of the meaning of kingdom. See his notes under Daniel 2:44, Zechariah 12:8, Matthew 3:2. Under Matthew 6:33 Scofield says,

> The expression, "the kingdom of God," although used in many cases as synonymous with the kingdom of heaven, is to be distinguished from it in some instances (see Matthew 3:2, note): (1) The kingdom of God is at times viewed as everlasting and universal, i.e., the rule of the sovereign God over all creatures and things (Ps. 103:19; Dan. 4:3). In this sense the kingdom of God includes the kingdom of heaven. (2) The kingdom of God is also used to designate the sphere of salvation entered only by the new birth (John 3:5-7) in contrast with the kingdom of heaven as the sphere of profession which may be real or false (see Matthew 13:3, note; 25:1, 11-12). And (3) since the kingdom of heaven is in the earthly sphere of the universal kingdom of God, the two have many things in common and in some contexts are interchangeable. "Like the kingdom of heaven, the kingdom of

God is realized in the rule of God in the present age and will also be fulfilled in the future millennial kingdom. It continues forever in the eternal state (cp. Dan. 4:3)."[11]

My own view is that the term *kingdom* is best defined as "the rule of God in the hearts of men."[12] Wherever Christ is received as Savior and Lord, wherever God's Word is preached and His will is obeyed, there in some small measure is the kingdom. The kingdom is not the Church, but the Church bears witness to the kingdom in this age. The kingdom is not the millennium, but the most nearly perfect earthly expression of the kingdom will take place during the millennium. The kingdom is not heaven, in heaven the kingdom will be perfected.

When Dispensationalists recognize that the term *kingdom* can have other references besides the Millennium, the term might cease to be a trigger word which brings unnecessary reactions.

(5) Law and Gospel

Luther divided Scripture into law and gospel. Law is not simply Old Testament and gospel is not simply New Testament; there is much gospel in the Old Testament and much law in the New Testament.

Luther's definition is simple and clear: The law says, This is what you must do for God. The gospel says, This is what God has done for you.

In relation to civil government, Luther's point is that rulers should apply the law and not the gospel, because they deal with a largely unregenerate society. Luther said the policy of the godly Christian prince toward evildoers should consist of "proper zeal and firmness." Notice he did not speak of mercy and turning the other cheek. The reason is that those principles govern individual believers in their relations with other people, not rulers in relation to their subjects. Romans 12, which speaks of forgiveness and not avenging wrongs, applies to the individual believer; Romans 13, which calls the civil magistrate God's "avenger" and a "terror to evil works" who "beareth not the sword in vain," is for rulers. The civil ruler has God-given authority to avenge wrongs and punish evildoers because he has a God-given responsibility to protect his people from evildoers, foreign and domestic. In my opinion a major failure of the Carter administration was that President Carter tried to conduct foreign policy according to gospel rather than law; he tried to govern according to Romans 12 when he should have governed according to Romans 13.

(6) Three Uses of Law

Luther and Calvin both said the law has three uses; civil, pedagogical, and didactic. The civil use occurs when governmental authorities take the principles of the law and enact them into statute to keep public order and protect human rights.

The pedagogical use occurs when the believer sees the timeless and perfect standard of righteousness found in the law, realizes his own sinfulness by comparison, and recognizes his need for grace through the atoning death of Jesus Christ on the Cross. (Gal. 3:24: "The law was our schoolmaster to bring us unto Christ.")

The didactic use occurs when believers study the law as a means of better understanding the will and character of God so that as believers through the power of the Holy Spirit they can conform their lives to His will.

Lutheran confirmation classes often refer to these three uses as the curb, the mirror, and the rule. Of these, the curb, or civil, use is most relevant to our discussion of law and government.

(7) Application of God's Law

The application of God's law to civil society is a complex and difficult question. Dispensationalists and Reconstructionists debate this issue, not only against each other but also within their own respective camps.

Each side tends to oversimplify the issue. To some Reconstructionists, God's law is God's law, over and out. After all, who but a heathen could be against the law of God?

Dispensationalists also tend to oversimplify the issue.

With a glib recitation of Paul's words, "We are not under law, but under grace" (Rom. 6:14-15), we leave the issue behind us and go our merry way as though the law is totally inapplicable today (except that we don't really act that way; if we did, we'd have to accept situation ethics, and most of us aren't willing to do that).

But what does it really mean to not be "under law"? First, it means keeping the law is not the means of our salvation. (It never was, but some of the Jews of Paul's day had distorted it into a means of salvation.) Second, it means we are no longer required to follow the ceremonial law—the temple rites, the sacrifices, etc. Third, it means we are not bound by extrabiblical taboos, whether the Jewish Talmud or the taboos of modern fundamentalist Christianity. (Many of these may be good disciplines to follow, so long as they are not viewed as a mark of salvation or spirituality.)

Paul did not mean the law has no relevance today. He said the law is "holy, just and good" (Rom. 7:12). The law reflects the character of God: His holiness, His justice, His righteousness. And since the character of God does not change (Heb. 13:8), His law does not change either. The law of God is a timeless standard against which the law of man must be measured.

While the Mosaic Covenant and its laws are binding as covenant law upon Israel alone, the timeless principles found in the law are valid for all nations. In Proverbs 14:34 we read, "Righteous exalteth a nation: but sin is a reproach to any people." In other words, God has established universal principles of right and wrong that apply not just to Israel but to "any people." Those nations which follow God's standards will receive His blessing; those which despise His standards will incur His judgment.

Israel's law was an example to other nations. As Moses said to Israel in Deuteronomy 6:5-8,

> Behold, I have taught you statutes and judgments, even as the Lord my God commanded me, that ye should do so in the land whither ye go to possess it.

Keep therefore and do them; for this is your wisdom and your understanding in the sight of the nations, which shall hear all these statutes, and say, Surely this great nation is a wise and understanding people.

For what nation is there so great, who hath God so nigh unto them, as the Lord our God is in all things that we call upon him for?

And what nation is there so great, that hate statutes and judgments so righteous as all this law, which I set before you this day?

Isaiah made a similar observation: "The isles shall wait for his law" (Isa. 42:4). The term *isles* normally refers to Gentile nations, and the Hebrew term for *law* used here means doctrine and can refer to both law and gospel.

Believing God's law has legitimate application for today is one thing; knowing how to apply it is another. Dr. House and Pastor Ice suggest that the Wisdom literature (Job, Psalms, Proverbs, Ecclesiastes, Song of Solomon) may be the key to this application.[13] This thought needs development but could be fruitful.

Those portions of the Old Testament that are part of the Noachic Covenant, the covenant God made with Noah in Genesis 9, are said to be binding upon all people, indeed all flesh, for perpetual generations (Gen. 9:12). They may thus be applied more literally than the Mosaic law, which as covenant applies only to Israel but which contains principles of universal application. But in both cases wise and considerate application is needed.

For example, in Genesis 1:28 God gave man dominion over the earth, and in Genesis 9:3 He authorized man to kill animals for food. Reconstructionists sometimes call this the "dominion mandate." But God also gave man a "stewardship mandate," a responsibility to take good care of the earth, using wise conservation practices (Gen. 2:15). As the legislature adopts hunting laws, it needs to consider both factors, giving people freedom to hunt for food but tempering this freedom with wise conservation practices.

This may result in different applications in different

areas. For example, moose are very rare in North Dakota. So North Dakota allows only a very limited hunting season for moose, and that only in a few eastern counties. Moose are much more plentiful in northern Minnesota and Manitoba, so these jurisdictions allow a more extended hunting season.

This does not mean God's law differs from North Dakota to Minnesota. The principles of the dominion mandate and the stewardship mandate are the same, but different circumstances require different applications.

And then we come to that most difficult subject, the law of nature. Paul says very plainly that Gentiles who had not heard the Word of God, still could not be excused for their sin because they had a basic knowledge of right and wrong, the working of the law of God written upon their hearts, or their consciences:

> For when the Gentiles, which have not the law, do by nature the things contained in the law, these, having not the law, are a law unto themselves; Which show the work of the law written in their hearts, their conscience also bearing witness, and their thoughts the mean while accusing or else excusing one another. (Rom. 2:14-15)

Jesus used the same principle to encourage people to ask God for help:

> Or what man is there of you, whom if his son ask bread, will he give him a stone? Or if he ask a fish, will he give him a serpent? If ye then, being evil, know how to give good gifts to your children, how much more shall your Father which is in heaven give good things to them that ask him? (Matt. 7:9-11)

The point is that even unregenerate, sinful men have a basic knowledge of how to be good parents, good citizens, good employees, and good neighbors. The reason is the law of God written upon their hearts, the law of nature.

We need a balanced view of the law of nature. Dr. Norman Geisler, a leading dispensational theologian formerly of Dallas Theological Seminary and now with Liberty University, says human government should be guided by the law of nature, not Scripture. He says Scripture is not binding on civil government; rather, civil government should follow the law of nature which is God's general revelation to all men.[14]

I respectfully disagree. In my opinion Dr. Geisler in his otherwise excellent article draws too sharp a dichotomy between the revealed law of Scripture and the law of nature. Both, he agrees, are part of the law of God. Therefore, I would think, they must be consistent. Scripture may address matters we cannot discern through nature, and there may be principles of the law of nature on which the Scriptures are silent. But since God is absolute truth, and truth cannot contradict itself, the law of God as revealed in Scripture and the law of God as revealed in nature cannot contradict. If they appear to conflict, we misinterpret one or the other, or both.

But if Dr. Geisler in his fear of applying Scripture is too quick to rely entirely on the law of nature, some Reconstructionists in their eagerness to apply Scripture are too quick to discount natural law. Dr. Gary DeMar suggests that natural law is not a good basis for governmental policy because since the Fall nature has become corrupt and man's ability to apprehend natural law has become equally corrupt.[15] He cites J. J. Packer to explain why an ethical system cannot be constructed from nature:

> One of the most revolting things I ever saw was one of our children's hamsters eating its young. Abortion, whereby a mother-to-be using medical personnel as her agents "eats up" the small person of whom she gets rid, is the human equivalent.[16]

I believe Dr. DeMar has confused the law of nature as expounded by Augustine, Aquinas, and others throughout church history, with natural law as understood by Thomas Hobbes. Hobbes saw natural law as that which was natural.

It is normal in nature for a creature to defend itself; therefore, the right of self-defense is a natural law. But in a
fallen world many things happen in nature which do not
provide a good ethical basis for men.

But that is not the way Christians have traditionally
understood the law of nature. In the traditional view, the
law of nature is God's general revelation to all men by
which He has given men a basic knowledge of right and
wrong. In this view the law of nature is what ought to be,
not what is as in the Hobbesian view. Sir William Blackstone,
for example, described the law of nature as "dictated by
God himself," but he acknowledged that because man's
reason is corrupted by the Fall he has difficulty understanding the law of nature. For that reason, he said, the
revealed law of Scripture takes precedence over the law of
nature—not because it is more of God, but because it is
more clear:

> Undoubtedly the revealed system is of infinitely
> more authenticity than that moral system, which is
> framed by ethical writers, and denominated the
> natural law. Because one is the law of nature, ex-
> pressly declared so to be by God Himself, the other
> is only what, by the assistance of human reason, we
> imagine to be that law. If we could be as certain of
> the latter as we are of the former, both would have
> an equal authority; but, till then, they can never be
> put in any competition together.[17]

A balanced view of the law of nature, then, sees that
law as of God but less clear than the law of Scripture.
Where the law of nature appears to conflict with the law
of Scripture—and it can be only an apparent conflict, because both are of God and God does not contradict Himself—the law of Scripture takes precedence.

Some have suggested that Luther did not believe in the
law of nature, but his writings reveal otherwise. He did not
write extensively on the subject, but I suggest the reason
is that his view of the law of nature differed little from that
of his Roman Catholic predecessors. In his letter on "Secu-

lar Authority" he clearly affirmed his belief in the law of
nature as a means of resolving disputes:

> But if neither is a Christian, or if either is unwilling
> to be judged by the law of love, you may ask them
> to call in another judge, and announce to them
> that they are acting against God and the law of
> nature, even though they may obtain absolute jus-
> tice through human law. For nature, like love,
> teaches that I should do as I would be done by. . . .
> Thus one should deal with all property unlawfully
> held, whether in public or private, that love and
> the law of nature may always prevail. For when you
> judge according to love, you will easily decide and
> adjust matters without any law-books. But when
> you ignore love and natural law, you will never
> succeed in pleasing God, though you have devoured
> all the law-books and jurists; they will only cause
> you to err, the more you depend on them.[18]

How, then, do we determine what is the law of nature?
Is it just what we "feel" to be right, or because that's the
way we've always done it? I am reminded of the Savage in
Aldous Huxley's *Brave New World* who insists that it is
natural to believe in God. Mustafa Mond, the Comptroller
of the "brave new world" superstate, answers, "You might
as well ask if it's natural to do up one's trousers with
zippers. . . . People believe in God because they've been
conditioned to believe in God."[19]

Universal assent is one means of apprehending the law
of nature. Luther's associate Philip Melanchthon wrote,

> The law of nature is the common opinion to which
> we all as men equally agree, and which God has
> engraved upon the heart of every one.[20]

But the heart or conscience of an individual and even
an entire society can become perverted and even demonic,
so this is not a totally reliable test. In looking for universal
assent it is wise to look not only at what is universally

accepted today, but also at what has been universally or at least widely accepted throughout the ages.

A second means of apprehending the law of nature is our God-given power of human logic and reason. Reason, of course, is fallible; but it is a God-given tool for discerning right from wrong and is of some value in determining the law of nature. The Enlightenment of the 1700s is often portrayed as a triumph of human reason over divine revelation, but this is a false dichotomy. Most of the Enlightenment thinkers were Christian, at least in their basic world view. The Puritan preachers of New England discoursed extensively upon the legitimate role of reason in the Christian faith. They considered reason not as evil but as a God-given tool for understanding truth. There was, of course, another wing of the Enlightenment which saw reason as self-contained within man and divorced from God. This led to each man being his own source of reason, which ultimately led to subjectivism (to every man his own truth, for reality is as you perceive it) and irrationalism.

A third question to ask in determining whether a proposed principle is truly the law of nature, is whether it is consistent with the character of God as we know Him from Scripture.

And a fourth consideration is whether it is consistent with the principles found in the Word of God. As we saw above, Blackstone emphasized that the law of nature cannot contradict the revealed law of Scripture.

I do not delude myself into thinking that I have solved every problem associated with applying the law of God; I have only begun to scratch the surface. But I hope I have led believers to recognize that the law of God does apply. The exact principles of application, and the implementation of those principles, is a matter for Christian reflection, Christian scholarship, Christian debate, and Christian prayer.

Conclusion

Dispensationalists and Reconstructionists have both made major contributions to Christian thought in recent years. In some ways the debate is helpful. My fear is that it will turn bitter as some individuals on both sides accuse the others of serving the Enemy.

Let me offer a few closing thoughts to both camps. First, the fundamentals of the faith have traditionally been recognized as the inspiration and authority of Scripture, the Trinity, the divine and human natures of Jesus Christ brought together in His virgin birth, substitutionary atonement, and the Second Coming of Christ. On these fundamentals Dispensationalists and Reconstructionists are in agreement, except that, while agreeing that Christ is coming again, they disagree on some of the surrounding details. There is no reason for either camp to charge the other with heresy or to refuse to accept each other as fellow believers.

I note particularly that a few Dispensationalists have accused Reconstructionists of being in league with the New Age movement. The basic principles of the New Age movement include (1) rejection of absolute reality and absolute morality; (2) an impersonal god (or goddess); (3) pantheism; (4) evolution; (5) man as an evolving animal is part of nature; (6) man is God; (7) man creates his own reality; (8) man's problem is separation from nature; (9) the solution is back to nature through divination, magic, mind control, altered states of consciousness, visualization, transcendental meditation, exercise, health food, spirit guides, etc.; and (10) man's ultimate destiny, the Age of Aquarius and the quantum evolutionary leap to the new Aquarian race. The Reconstructionist authors I have mentioned above—Rushdoony, Bahnsen, DeMar, North, and others—are diametrically opposed to each and every one of these principles. In fact, Gary North's book *Unholy Spirits: Occultism and New Age Humanism* (Ft. Worth: Dominion Press, 1986) is the best book exposing the New Age movement to date. Traditional Christian Reconstructionists are as far from the New Age movement as one could get.

However, I must warn my Reconstructionist brethren that there is danger in the camp. Some of the new elements which have recently entered the reconstruction movement—and the movement has become an unusual alliance of old-line Calvinists and new-line charismatics—

could have dangerous tendencies. Within the movement today are some who have stretched dominion to the point of "name it and claim it" and some who advocate visualization and other New Age practices to achieve their goals. This is not a problem endemic to Christian reconstruction; these persons would probably hold these heretical ideas with or without the reconstruction movement, because they derived those ideas from other sources. But they are a danger to watch out for nevertheless.

And another danger: The dominion mandate can be appealing to those who want power for themselves. Again, this is not inherent with reconstruction; it is an aberration to watch out for. It is important for Reconstructionists to resist the temptation to pride. The fact that God has revealed His law to us in His Word should humble us and cause us to realize our own inability to find it ourselves. Instead, it can make us proud and cause us to think of ourselves as God's special spokesmen. Pray for humility!

And now, a word to my fellow Dispensationalists. Reconstructionists are carefully studying God's Word and its application to the problems of contemporary society. They are developing a comprehensive Reconstructionist world view. It is essential that Dispensationalists address themselves to the problems of our day, applying godly solutions from a dispensational standpoint. Otherwise, Christians will be forced to choose between the Reconstructionist position and the Humanist position. If neither of these is satisfactory, develop an alternative!

Finally, a word of admonition for all of us. We live in a world of great adversity. Communism, despite its current disarray, still controls much of the world. The third world is fraught with militant Islam, demonism, socialism, liberation theology, and other competing forces. Our own sector, known as the Free World, is rocked with competing ideologies: liberalism, secular humanism, the New Age, Satanism, permissivism, welfarism, statism, and the like.

Dispensationalists and Reconstructionists: On every level and on every front, we are in a battle for the hearts, minds, and souls of men. Don't we have better things to do besides fighting each other?

These [Bereans] were more noble than those in Thessalonica, in that they received the word with all readiness of mind, and searched the scriptures daily, whether those things were so. (Acts 17:11)

Notes to Appendix

1 A newsletter called the "New Age Adversary Bulletin" (February 1988) recently referred to "Christian Reconstructionists like Dr. John Eidsmoe and Peter Marshall Jr." Since in the preceding paragraph the author wrote that "Christian Reconstructionists/Dominion Theology/Kingdom Now people all take the post-millennial view," I naively assumed that if I could show the author the many passages in my books where I affirm my premillennial and dispensational position, he would retract. No such luck. Rather, in the March 1988 issue he changed his definition of reconstruction, saying "a few Christian Reconstructionists take the pre-millennial view." Reading his reply, I could only shake my head and recall Humpty Dumpty in Lewis Carroll's *Through the Looking Glass:* "When I use a word, it means exactly what I want it to mean, nothing more and nothing less."

2 Many Dispensationalists believe that current events, particularly the rise of apostasy and the rebirth of the State of Israel, indicate that the return of Jesus Christ is near and that we are living in the Last Days. I believe this is a distinct possibility but by no means certain. Many ages have interpreted the Scriptures to mean the Lord was coming in their lifetimes.

3 Rousas J. Rushdoony, *The Biblical Philosophy of History* (Phillipsburg, NJ: Presbyterian & Reformed, 1979), 16.

4 Norman Geisler, "A Premillennial View of Law and Government," *Moody Monthly,* October 1985.

5 In my book *The Christian Legal Advisor* (Grand Rapids: Baker Book House, 1984, 1987), I devote fourteen chapters to the First Amendment and its ramifications for Christians.

6 Martin Luther, "Secular Authority: To What Extent It Should Be Obeyed," 1523; *Works of Martin Luther* (Grand Rapids: Baker, 1982), 3:237.

7 Ibid., 270-271.

8 Lewis Sperry Chafer, *Systematic Theology* (Dallas: Dallas Seminary Press, 1948, 1976), 7:223.

9 John F. Walvoord, *Jesus Christ Our Lord* (Chicago: Moody, 1969, 1987), 134-35.

10 J. Dwight Pentecost, *Things to Come* (Grand Rapids: Zondervan, 1964, 1978), 427-475.

11 C. I. Scofield, *The New Scofield Reference Bible* (New York: Oxford University Press, 1969), see Matthew 6:33.

12 My views on the meaning of the kingdom were derived from many sources. One in particular was *A Theology of the New Testament* by George Eldon Ladd, a nondispensational premillennialist (Grand Rapids: Eerdmans, 1974, 1977).

13 Wayne House and Thomas Ice, *Dominion Theology: Blessing or Curse* (Portland: Multnomah, 1988), 186-88.

14 Geisler, "A Premillennial View."

15 Gary DeMar, *The Debate Over Christian Reconstruction* (Atlanta: American Vision Press, 1988), 65-67.

16 J. I. Packer, "It's Wrong to Eat People," *Christianity Today* (8 April 1988): 11; quoted in Ibid., 66.

17 Sir William Blackstone, *Commentaries*, ed. Jones, 1765; quoted in Eidsmoe, *The Christian Legal Advisor*, 41-42.

18 Luther, *Works of Martin Luther*, 3:272.

19 Aldous Huxley, *Brave New World* (New York: Bantam, 1939, 1962), 159.

20 Philip Melanchthon, *Loci Communes*, 1521; cited in Luther, *Works of Martin Luther*, 3:272.